T0196388

A Simple Will *for* Dying Well

How to Handwrite Your Own
Will WITHOUT Witnesses,
Notaries, or Lawyers.

Jay H. Turner III, Esq.

Archway Publishing books may be ordered through booksellers or by contacting:

Archway Publishing
1663 Liberty Drive
Bloomington, IN 47403
www.archwaypublishing.com
1 (888) 242-5904

ISBN: 978-1-4808-5711-7 (sc)
ISBN: 978-1-4808-5710-0 (hc)
ISBN: 978-1-4808-5712-4 (e)

Library of Congress Control Number: 2018900244

Print information available on the last page.

Archway Publishing rev. date: 01/12/2018

In this world nothing can be said to be certain,
except death and taxes.
—Benjamin Franklin

Dedication

To my children, Hugh, Helen and Bowen, who have taught me to love unconditionally.

Disclaimer

While best efforts have been used in writing this book, the publisher and author make no representations or warranties of any kind and assume no liabilities of any kind with respect to the accuracy or completeness of the contents and specifically disclaim any implied warranties of merchantability or fitness of use for a particular purpose. Neither the author nor the publisher shall be held liable or responsible to any person or entity with respect to any loss, incidental or consequential damages caused, or alleged to have been caused, directly or indirectly, by the information contained in or omitted by this book. By reading or using this book, you agree to this release of liability.

Although the author is a lawyer, reading this book does not create an attorney-client relationship between you and the author. This book provides a general review of estate planning issues, but should not be used as a substitute for the advice of a competent attorney admitted or authorized to practice in your state.

Contents

Chapter 1

Why Have a Will?

The only guarantees in life are an eventual death and, as Ben Franklin points out, the need to pay some taxes along the way. Despite the certainty of our own mortality, most people in America have not prepared a will. In a Gallup poll taken in 2016,[1] only 44 percent of Americans reported having prepared a will. This is lower than in two prior Gallup polls: 51 percent in 2005 and 48 percent in 1990. According to the statistics, approximately 56 percent of Americans will die intestate (a legal term for "without a will"). Such people come from all income and socioeconomic levels. The recent death of the musician Prince is but one high-profile example of a person with significant assets who died without a will. In Prince's case, the lack of a will opened the door for numerous "heirs" claiming to be his wife, child, sibling, and other distant relatives. Without a will identifying beneficiaries, his estate will undoubtedly incur additional and significant legal costs addressing these claims.

The statistics are discouraging, and they mean that most families will, at some point, administer an intestate estate. When a person dies without a will, the state laws of his or her residence determine who inherits the estate assets. The people who inherit are referred to as the "heirs at law." The heirs at law generally start with the closest

---

[1] http://www.gallup.com/poll/191651/majority-not.aspx.

living relatives and then move out along family lines. Sometimes this arrangement works fine, but other times not.

It would be interesting to do a survey of Americans who would be willing to let their state government mandate exactly how they could spend their money during their lifetimes. I suspect the number who would be willing to do that would be very small. But by dying without a will, such individuals are doing just that: allowing the state to determine to whom their assets pass at death. Moreover, these estates are significantly more difficult and expensive to administer than when a decedent prepared a will.

One common worry is that if a person dies without a will, the state will take that person's assets. Although this result is unlikely, it is possible, depending on state law and whether the person left behind any close surviving relatives. Even if there are living heirs at law, such heirs may not be the beneficiaries that the decedent intended to benefit. There are several common scenarios that result in unintended inheritance situations.

✓ **Multiple marriages**. If the surviving spouse is not the mother or father of all of the decedent's children, many states require that part of the estate pass immediately to the children. Logically, this makes sense. If the surviving spouse inherited everything, then there is a good chance that his or her stepchild—the decedent's child—would not later inherit anything. This is a good law if you are a child but not a great law if you are the surviving spouse. For example, I handled an estate where the wife died unexpectedly without preparing a will. The wife had two children from a prior marriage, and under state law, all of her assets, including her house, were divided between her second husband and her two children. At her death, her husband and children then became co-owners of the family home, and no matter how good the relationship between children and stepparents are, no spouse wants to lose the exclusive right to live in the family home.

✓ **Underage beneficiaries**. Without a will, a parent cannot make any provisions for a minor child. When a minor child inherits assets under state law, that child will normally gain full access to those assets upon reaching the age of majority (typically age eighteen). I witnessed an eighteen-year-old inherit a large sum of money, and instead of going back to college, the newly rich "adult" embarked on other plans for his time and money. This resulted in tragic, life-altering, bad decisions on his part. A far better result might have come about if someone had been named to hold the assets on the child's behalf until he reached a more appropriate age. The will is also the document in which parents nominate guardians for minor children. Without a will, the court must decide who takes custody of minor children, which can result in fights over who takes possession of the children.

✓ **Nonheir beneficiaries**. Without a will, a fiancé, stepchild, or other person you may intend to treat as family will not inherit under the intestacy statutes. For example, if you wanted to leave assets to your best friend, it is very unlikely that your friend would inherit anything under your state intestacy laws.

✓ **Lack of control**. Without a will, you give up the right to appoint the person who will administer your estate (known as the "executor"). This opens the gates for various persons (possibly including creditors) to seek appointment and control the disposition of your estate.

✓ **Additional costs**. Not having a will can also cause your estate and beneficiaries to incur significant expenses. If you do not have close relatives, or you have several distant relatives who might inherit, your estate may have to hire a geological search firm and/or seek court approval to determine who inherits. I worked on an estate where the heirs were very distant cousins, and the family tree ended up being the size of a large conference table. I have also seen a large estate where a father's purported long-lost child appeared after the father's death, claiming inheritance rights. This required multiple court hearings and ultimately a DNA test. Clearly, this process can have significant costs to the family, monetarily and emotionally.

So for all the reasons discussed here, if you are one of the majority of Americans without a will, I hope this book will give you the information and motivation necessary to change that.

Chapter 2

Handwritten (Holographic) Wills

A holographic will is a will that is solely in the handwriting of the person creating the will. The only requirement, in most states, is that the signature and the material parts of the will be in the person's handwriting. There are some key advantages to creating a handwritten will. One of the most significant advantages is simplicity. There is no need for an attorney, a notary, or even a witness to make a valid will—just an individual, a pen, and a paper. This is unlike typewritten wills or wills prepared through an online service, which require two (or more) witnesses to be present when the person signs the will. Another advantage to a handwritten will is cost. The will can be prepared without legal fees or subscription costs to online services.

Although there are numerous books on wills and estate planning in general, this book specifically gives individuals the information and skills necessary to handwrite a valid will.

There are several low-cost providers of online "simple" wills, and these wills can be appropriate in certain situations. However, many of the wills procured online that I have seen have not been signed and witnessed with the formalities required for typewritten wills. If these formalities are not followed exactly, a typewritten will may not be valid at a person's death. For example, in my home state of Virginia, for a typewritten will to be valid, it must be willingly signed and executed in the presence two witnesses, and the two witnesses and the person signing must be in the presence of each other at the time of signing. Several years ago, I was helping a family whose father had died after preparing a will online. I was required to track down one of the witnesses to confirm that the will had been executed properly. After several internet searches, I was able to track the witness down. We spoke, and I asked her about the will in hopes that she would remember signing it. I went through a list of questions with her on the telephone.

Me: "Thank you for taking my call. Do you remember Mr. Smith?"

Witness: "Yes, I do."

Me: "Do you remember being a witness to Mr. Smith's will?"

Witness: "Yes, I remember distinctly that he came into the bank one day, and one of the tellers and I witnessed his will."

Me: "Perfect. Last question: were you and the teller in the presence of Mr. Smith when he signed the will?"

Witness: "No. We were not. The bank manager took Mr. Smith into his office first and then brought the signed will out for us to witness. Is that a problem?"

In fact, it was a problem, and with these facts, the court refused to accept the will for probate. The great thing about handwritten wills is that there are none of these signing formalities, no need to hire an attorney, and no need to bother neighbors or bank tellers to be witnesses.

A potential downside to a handwritten will is that after a person's death, a state may require one or more persons to identify the handwriting as being that of the decedent. This is different from witnessing the will itself. This just requires independent verification that the handwriting in the will is in fact the decedent's handwriting. In some states, this validation can be provided by any person who is familiar with the person's handwriting. In others (e.g., Virginia), the witnesses of the decedent's handwriting must be disinterested witnesses (i.e., individuals who take nothing under the will). I will say, in my experience, when presented with a holographic will after a person's death, I have always (so far) been able to find witnesses to validate the handwriting.

A practical limitation to handwritten wills is that such wills are currently allowed in only roughly half the states. These states include the following:

Alaska
Arizona
Arkansas
California
Colorado
Hawaii
Idaho
Kentucky
Maine
Michigan
Mississippi
Montana
Nebraska
Nevada
New Jersey
North Carolina if found after death in a place intended for safekeeping)
North Dakota
Oklahoma
Pennsylvania
South Dakota
Tennessee
Texas
Utah
Virginia
West Virginia
Wyoming

So if you live in a state that is *not* on this list, you will not be able to handwrite a valid will without having witnesses at the time you sign. If you typewrite or use a preprinted version of a will, I cannot stress enough the importance of having the will witnessed correctly. If you use an online provider for your will, closely follow the signing instructions provided by the service. One benefit to using an attorney (in addition to getting one-on-one advice) is that your attorney will make sure your will signing is performed correctly. Regardless of what path you choose, this book will help clarify the various options provided by the online will providers or will help you work with an attorney to have your will professionally prepared.

Handwritten wills are not appropriate for complex estate planning. If you have a large estate with asset levels that could trigger an estate tax (state or federal), you will want to have estate planning done by an estate planning attorney. This generally means that if you have more than $5 million in assets or live in a state with a smaller estate tax or inheritance tax level (see appendix 2), you should have an attorney help you with your estate planning. Likewise, if you have a family member with special needs (mental or physical), you should talk to an attorney about special estate planning for that beneficiary.

Overall, I believe that for most of adults a handwritten will can be a simple, cost-effective solution for avoiding intestacy. If, after reading this book, you decide to hire an attorney or go online to prepare your will, the next few chapters will save you significant time and effort in that process. With most attorneys charging well over $200 an hour, this book's cost is but a small fraction of the savings you can reap in preparing your own will.

I also believe that estate planning is much like anything else in life: the more time and effort you put into it, the better your results will be. By spending a few hours with this book, you will be educating yourself on how to save your family and loved ones additional stress and expense at your death.

Chapter 3

Drafting the Will—
Introductory Paragraphs

In this chapter, I will go through the common introductory provisions of a will and provide sample language that can be used in handwriting your own will.

Introduction. The introductory provisions of the will contain your formal name and city and state of residence. You should use your full legal name, not your nickname or what you may go by socially. It is okay to use just a middle initial, rather than a full middle name, but if you have a common name (such as John Smith), I would spell out the middle name. Also, if you have changed your name recently or have any assets that are held in a former name, it is helpful to have a "formerly known as" designation to your old name. The introductory paragraph also contains a sentence that revokes any prior wills or codicils (amendments to a will) that you may have previously enacted. That language is important because you want your will to be self-contained entirely within one document. This provision also emphasizes the importance of dating your will each time you do one.

Family. The next paragraph defines your family members and whether you are married, single, or divorced. Here I like to identify children or other close relatives who may be referenced in the will. By defining children, you greatly decrease the likelihood of a purported long-lost child surfacing and attempting to inherit your estate after your death.

Blended families. There has been a large increase in families that are considered "blended"—where one or both spouses have children from prior relationships. Sometimes the stepchildren are adopted by a stepparent (which I will discussed later), and other times they are not. If the intent is for all children to be treated equally, that should be clearly stated in the introductory paragraph.

Introduction Language

> ## Last Will and Testament
> ### of
> ### Samantha P. Sample
>
> I, Samantha P. Sample, of City, State, on this ___ day of _____ 2017, being of sound mind, do hereby make this my Last Will and Testament. I revoke all other wills and codicils I have previously made.

Family Language: Married with Children

> ## Family
>
> I am married to Elizabeth M. Sample ("my spouse"). I have two children, Sam P. Sample Jr. and Sarah L. Sample (these children and any other children born to or adopted by me shall be individually known as "my child" and collectively known as "my children").

Family Language: Second Marriage Where Stepchildren Will Inherit

Family

I am married to Elizabeth M. Sample ("my spouse"). I have two children from a prior marriage, Sam P. Sample Jr. and Sarah L. Sample. My wife has two children from a prior marriage, Benjamin D. Smith and Samantha S. Smith. Sam P. Sample Jr., Sarah L. Sample, Benjamin D. Smith, and Samantha S. Smith shall each be individually referred to herein as "my child" and collectively as "my children."

Family Language: Second Marriage Where Stepchildren Do Not Inherit

Family

I am married to Elizabeth M. Sample ("my spouse"). I have two children from a prior marriage, Sam P. Sample Jr. and Sarah L. Sample. My wife has two children from a prior marriage, Benjamin D. Smith and Samantha S. Smith. Only Sam P. Sample Jr. and Sarah L. Sample shall be individually referred to herein as "my child" and collectively as "my children."

Family Language: Single, Widowed, or Divorced with Children

Family

I am widowed [or divorced or single]. I have two children, Sam P. Sample Jr. and Sarah L. Sample (these children and any other children born to or adopted by me shall be individually known as "my child" and collectively known as "my children").

Family Language: Single, Widowed, or Divorced without Children

Family

I am single (or divorced or widowed). I have no descendants who survive me.

Chapter 4

Drafting the Will—Tangible Personal Property

The next few chapters will focus on dispositive provisions of the will—or, more simply, how to give away your assets at your death.

I address tangible personal property in a separate paragraph in the will. Tangible personal property includes items such as jewelry, clothing, china, cars, furniture, and other household goods. It also includes pets, which I discuss in detail later. One word of warning: there seems to be a common myth that placing a person's name on an item in the house somehow mandates that the item pass to that named person at your death. That is very unlikely and can cause a lot of confusion and possible conflicts between the "named" person and the actual beneficiary. If you want an item to go to a certain person, you are much better off including a specific bequest of that item in your will. Most states also allow you to create a separate list to identify items and to whom they will pass at you death (i.e., this is a list that is made independent of your will and is mentioned in the will only as being in existence). See appendix 3 for the states that allow you to make a list of items. In most states, the list must be signed and dated by you. The nice aspect of a list is that you can make it at any time and can change it at any time, without having to change your will.

If you make such a list, it should be on a separate sheet of paper and should specifically identify the items and persons who should receive them. This list may be changed by you from time to time, without a change to your will. Remember that you cannot give away real property, cash, stocks, or bonds by using a list—only tangible personal property can be gifted this way. Although the list can be typewritten or handwritten, in keeping with the theme of this book, I suggest that you handwrite the document if you are handwriting your will.

I discourage clients from trying to give away *all* their personal items by using the list. In other words, do not make a multipage list itemizing every item of personal property in your house or apartment. That approach tends to greatly complicate the administration of the estate since, inevitably, some item on the list will go missing, will be sold, or will otherwise be disposed of before you die. If you live in one of the states that do not allow the use of a list, you still can make specific bequests of personal property within the will itself.

The will should address what happens to the personal property remaining after the specific gifts are made. In many cases, the remaining tangible personal property will be divided among several beneficiaries. There is a scene in the movie *Fargo* where two of the characters discuss the challenge of "splitting" a car between themselves. That scene ended badly, and this can be a very real issue when trying to divide tangibles among beneficiaries. I usually give the executor the authority to divide the tangibles among the beneficiaries as may be practical given the nature of the assets. Hopefully, the beneficiaries can agree among themselves as to an appropriate division, but I include a method of division in the will in case they do not.

If you have young children, you should also include language addressing what happens if a young child inherits tangible personal property. Also, you may own items that will not make sense to hold for the benefit of a child. For example, it would not make sense to hold a car for the benefit of a six-year-old. Rather, it would make sense for the executor to sell the car and invest the net proceeds of the sale for the benefit of the child. If you have young children, I suggest giving the executor the authority to sell items of tangible personal property and to add the net proceeds of such sale to the residue of the estate (which can be held for the minor child's benefit).

Tangible Personal Property: Married, No List, Minor Children

Tangible Personal Property. I give all my tangible personal property to my spouse, if my spouse survives me. If my spouse does not survive me, I give all my remaining tangible personal property in as nearly equal shares as my Executor deems practical to my children who survive me; it is provided that my Executor may sell any such tangible personal property that my Executor may deem inappropriate for distribution in kind and add the net proceeds of sale to my residuary estate.

My Executor may distribute tangible personal property passing to a minor beneficiary to an adult person with whom a minor resides, and that adult person's receipt shall be a sufficient voucher in the accounts of my Executor.

Tangible Personal Property: Married, No List, Adult Children

Tangible Personal Property. I give all my tangible personal property to my spouse, if my spouse survives me. If my spouse does not survive me, my Executor shall distribute my remaining tangible personal property to my children who survive me in as nearly equal shares as may be agreed upon by my children or, in the absence of such an agreement, as determined by my Executor in his or her sole discretion.

Tangible Personal Property: Married, List, Minor Children

Tangible Personal Property. I may make a written list expressing how I wish certain items of my tangible personal property to be distributed. In such event, I direct that the list be given effect under the laws of the state of my residence at my death.

I give my remaining tangible personal property to my spouse, if my spouse survives me. If my spouse does not survive me, I give my remaining tangible personal property in as nearly equal shares as my Executor deems practical to my children who survive me; it is provided that my Executor may sell any such tangible personal property that my Executor may deem inappropriate for distribution in kind and add the net proceeds of sale to my residuary estate.

My Executor may distribute tangible personal property passing to a minor beneficiary to an adult person with whom a minor resides, and that adult person's receipt shall be a sufficient voucher in the accounts of my Executor.

Tangible Personal Property: Married, List, Adult Children

Tangible Personal Property. I may make a written list expressing how I wish certain items of my tangible personal property to be distributed. In such event, I direct that the list be given effect under the laws of the state of my residence at my death.

I give my remaining tangible personal property to my spouse, if my spouse survives me. If my spouse does not survive me, the Executor shall distribute my remaining tangible personal property to my children who survive me in as nearly equal shares as may be agreed upon by my children or, in the absence of such an agreement, as determined by my Executor in his or her sole discretion.

Tangible Personal Property: Single/Widowed/Divorced, List, Adult Children

Tangible Personal Property. I may make a written list expressing how I wish certain items of my tangible personal property to be distributed. In such event, I direct that the list be given effect under the laws of the state of my residence at my death.

The Executor shall distribute my remaining tangible personal property to my children who survive me in as nearly equal shares as may be agreed upon by my children or, in the absence of such an agreement, as determined by my Executor in his or her sole discretion.

Tangible Personal Property: Single/Widowed/Divorced, List, Siblings

Tangible Personal Property. I may make a written list expressing how I wish certain items of my tangible personal property to be distributed. In such event, I direct that the list be given effect under the laws of the state of my residence at my death.

The Executor shall distribute my remaining tangible personal property to my siblings who survive me in as nearly equal shares as may be agreed upon by my siblings or, in the absence of such an agreement, as determined by my Executor in his or her sole discretion.

Tangible Personal Property: Single/Widowed/Divorced, List, Remaining Tangibles Sold

Tangible Personal Property. I may make a written list expressing how I wish certain items of my tangible personal property to be distributed. In such event, I direct that the list be given effect under the laws of the state of my residence at my death. I direct that my Executor sell my remaining items of tangible personal property and add the net proceeds of sale to my residuary estate.

Tangible Personal Property: Single/Widowed/Divorced, No List, Specific Bequests, Remaining Tangibles Sold

Tangible Personal Property.

1. I give my dining room table to my brother, RALPH S. SAMPLE, if he

survives me, and if he does not, this gift shall lapse.

2. I give my Royal Doulton china, tapestry pattern, to my friend, RICHARD D. SAMPLE, if he survives me, and if he does not, this gift shall lapse.

I direct that my Executor sell my remaining tangible personal property and add the net proceeds of sale to my residuary estate.

Form for List of Tangibles (for States That Allow List)

List Disposing of Items of Tangible Personal Property

I have executed this list to dispose of the items of tangible personal property set forth below. If any named beneficiary listed below does not survive me, the gift to such beneficiary shall lapse. If any of the following items are not owned by me at the time of my death, the gift of such item shall be deemed to be canceled. I give the following items of tangible personal property to the persons named below:

Name of Beneficiary   Description of Gift

_____   _____

_____   _____

_____   _____

_____   _____

_____   _____

_____   _____

Chapter 5

Drafting the Will—Specific Bequests of Cash

You may want to leave specific sums of money to certain individuals and/or charities. There are a few things to consider in doing this. First, what do you want to happen if the beneficiary of the cash bequest does not survive you? There are generally two ways to address this decision.

One approach is to require that the person survive you to receive the money. Another approach is to allow the bequest to be paid to the person's descendants (typically children) if the person does not survive you. This is typically done by attaching the term *per stirpes* to the bequest. *Per stirpes* means "by representation" (i.e., if a person predeceases you but has two children who survive you, that person's children would equally split the bequest). Please note that a beneficiary's spouse does not inherit under a *per stirpes* designation.

If you are making a bequest to a charity, please try to include as much identifying information as possible. You do not want your executor trying to figure out which charity you meant to benefit. For example, a gift to the "heart association" might be interpreted to mean any number of charities that support heart health. You should also address what the executor should do if the charity is no longer in existence at your death.

In making a specific bequest, it is good practice to both (1) spell out the amount that is going to the beneficiary and (2) include the alphanumeric number in parentheses following the spelled-out number. This cuts down on ambiguities and possible challenges. Note that if there is a difference between the written number and the alphanumeric number, the written number will typically control.

Specific bequests are fine for small cash bequests to individuals and charities. Do not attempt to give away all, or even most, of your assets through specific bequests! Some clients overestimate the cash and other liquid assets they will have at death, and the actual amount they die with can vary greatly after the will is signed. If in your will you give more away than you own, this can lead to your estate having to sell assets that you may not have intended to be sold and/or lead to only the partial fulfillment of other gifts. There can be significant complications in the administration of your estate if you give more in specific bequests than the sum of cash left in the estate at your death.

Also, I advise against making specific bequests of specific brokerage or bank accounts. Inevitably, the account numbers change over time, and/or the bank or brokerage firms change names, creating ambiguities as to what accounts were intended. If you want a specific account to go to a specific person, I believe it is safer to add a transfer on death ("TOD") or payable on death ("POD") designation to that account. You can contact your bank or brokerage firm to place a TOD (typically placed on security accounts) or POD (typically placed on bank accounts) on your accounts, and such designation will ensure that the specific account will pass directly to the intended beneficiary at your death.

Specific Bequests of Cash to Individuals

> Specific Bequests. I make the following specific bequests at my death:
>
> 1. Fifteen Thousand Dollars ($15,000) to PATRICIA SAMPLE, per stirpes.

2. Ten Thousand Dollars ($10,000) to JONATHAN SAMPLE, if he survives me, and if he does not, this gift shall lapse.

Specific Bequests of Cash to Charities

Specific Bequests. I make the following specific bequests at my death:

1. Ten Thousand Dollars ($10,000) to the Powhatan County Free Clinic, Powhatan County, Virginia, tax ID #01-23456.
2. Ten Thousand Dollars ($10,000) to the Richmond Metro YMCA, Richmond, Virginia, tax ID #01-23457.

If any charitable beneficiary named above is not in existence at my death, my Executor shall distribute the bequest to such other charity or charities my Executor shall select that, in the sole discretion of my Executor, most closely satisfy my original charitable intent.

Chapter 6

Drafting the Will—Specific Devise of Real Estate

You may also make a specific bequest of real property at death. Real property includes all residences—that is, the primary residence and any other homes or apartments or other real estate owned by you. To make this bequest, you identify the real property along with the person or persons to whom you want the real property to pass. As with other bequests, you will want to identify whether the distribution of real property will lapse or go to the person's descendants (*per stirpes*) should the beneficiary predecease you.

You may also want to have the executor sell all or a portion of the real estate and distribute the net proceeds to the desired beneficiaries. This might be a very desirable approach when you have several children, or other beneficiaries, who would inherit the property together. Multiple owners of one piece of property is rarely a good idea because there is rarely a unified vision for the property's use. Each owner may have individual rights in the property, but no one individual can sell or occupy the property exclusively.

There is one thing to note about using a specific devise ("gift") of real property. Some states have a rule that says if you make a specific devise of the real property, that real property passes to the beneficiary *subject to all mortgages that may be on the property*. In other words, if you leave your house to your child, that child will inherit that house and any debt (mortgage) on the house. That may or may not be want you want. If you want the mortgage to be paid by the estate and to have the real estate pass debt-free to the beneficiary, you should note this clearly in the will.

Occasionally, a client may wish to leave a life estate in a residence to a beneficiary. This type of planning allows a person (called the "life tenant") to live in the residence for his or her lifetime, and then at the life tenant's death, the residence passes to the ultimate beneficiaries (called "remaindermen"). This type of planning can be very complicated, and there are many issues that need to be considered. For example, how are the taxes, insurance, home repairs, and costs of capital improvements to the property to be split between the life tenant and remaindermen? What happens if the life tenant should move out of the house and into a nursing home? If you want to create a life estate in a beneficiary, you should discuss this with an attorney in your state.

Real Estate: Devise to Individual; If Not Living, to the Individual's Descendants

> Real Property. I give and devise my real property located at 123 Main Street, Richmond, Virginia, to my son, Randolph Sample, if he survives me, and if he does not, to his descendants who survive me, per stirpes. My Executor shall pay all debt secured by this real property, and the property shall pass free of any mortgage or other encumbrance.

Real Estate: Devise to Individual; If Not Living, Gift Lapses

> Real Property. I give and devise my real property located at 123 Main Street, Richmond, Virginia, to my son, Randolph Sample, if he survives me, and if he does not, this gift shall lapse. My Executor shall pay all debt secured by this real property, and the property shall pass free of any mortgage or other encumbrance.

Real Estate: Devise to Spouse; If Not Living, to Surviving Children

> Real Property. I give and devise my real property located at 123 Main Street, Richmond, Virginia, to my spouse, if she survives me, and if she does not, in equal shares to my children who survive me.

Real Estate: Devise to Spouse; If Not Living, Gift Lapses

> Real Property. I give and devise my real property, wherever located, to my spouse, if my spouse survives me. If my spouse does not survive me, this devise shall lapse.

Real Estate: Devise to Spouse; If Not Living, Real Estate Sold

Real Property. I give and devise my real property, wherever located, to my spouse, if my spouse survives me. If my spouse does not survive me, I direct that my Executor sell my real property, wherever located, and add the net proceeds of sale to my residuary estate.

Real Estate: Sold at Death

Real Property. I direct that my Executor sell my real property, wherever located, and add the net proceeds of sale to my residuary estate.

Chapter 7

Drafting the Will—Residue of the Estate

Once you have selected what specific bequests you would like to make (if any), the will *must* contain a residuary clause. A residuary clause is a catchall clause that distributes the property remaining after distribution of the specific bequests. Among the holographic wills I have reviewed over the years, the primary drafting issue I have noticed is the improper drafting of the residuary clause. The residuary clause language does not need to be complicated, but there are several variables to consider in drafting this clause.

Occasionally, I will talk to a person who has decided not to leave anything to his or her spouse. For example, if the spouses are both on their second or subsequent marriages, they sometimes want their assets just to go to their own children. If you are of that mind-set (or have some other reason for not wanting to leave anything to your spouse), note that most states have laws giving spouses certain rights over estate assets at death. In some states, this is automatically a right; in other states, the spouse must make an election to receive assets. Most states also allow spouses to enter into premarital (before married) or postmarital (after married) agreements to address these issues. Because these laws are complex and vary greatly from state to state, if you want to disinherit a spouse (even if it is a mutual decision), you will want to talk to an attorney in your state.

Another provision that clients sometimes ask about is whether to include a "no contest" provision in the will. Such a provision provides that should a beneficiary contest the validity of the will, that beneficiary will no longer be eligible to inherit under the will. That sounds simple enough, but it is anything but that in real life. One significant hurdle to these types of provisions is that they are not allowed in many states. And in the states where they are, the courts strictly construe them, meaning that if they are not clearly drafted, they will not be enforced as intended. In my experience, will contests are rare, especially if you prepared a well-thought-out, complete will. Therefore, I generally advise against including these types of provisions in a will.

Clients also occasionally ask whether they can limit a bequest to a person to encourage or discourage some action. For example, a client asked whether he could give his daughter $50,000—but only if she agreed not to marry a specific individual. I advise against creating such limitations for a variety of reasons, one being that courts often deem such restrictions void for being against public policy. So although you have broad latitude in determining who inherits, you do not have unlimited authority to influence behavior.

If you want to leave all or part of your estate to charity, consider whether you want to limit the charity's use of the funds. Generally, a charitable gift can be used for the charity's "general charitable purposes," but you could be more specific if appropriate (e.g., for the charity's endowment fund, building fund, or other specific use).

Residue: To Spouse; If Not Living, to Children

> Residue of Estate. After payment of my debts and estate administration expenses as provided herein, I give the residue of my real and personal property ("my residuary estate") to my spouse, if she survives me. If my spouse does not survive me, my

Executor shall divide my residuary estate into equal shares, one share for each of my children who survives me and one share for each of my children who predeceases me and who leaves one or more descendants who survive me. The share for a surviving child shall be distributed to such child, outright and free of trust. The share for the descendants of a deceased child shall be distributed to such deceased child's descendants, per stirpes.

Residue: To Siblings; If Not Living, to Nieces and Nephews

Residue of Estate. After payment of my debts and estate administration expenses as provided herein, I direct my Executor to divide and distribute the residue of my real and personal property ("my residuary estate") into equal shares, one share for each of my siblings who survives me and one share for each of my siblings who predeceases me and leaves one or more descendants who survive me. The Executor shall distribute the share for a living sibling to such sibling, outright and free of trust. My Executor shall distribute the share created for a deceased sibling to such sibling's living descendants, per stirpes.

Residue: To Charities

Residue of Estate. After payment of my debts and estate administration expenses as provided herein, I give the residue of my real and personal property ("my residuary estate") to the following:

1.   The Powhatan County Free Clinic, Powhatan County, Virginia, tax ID #01-23456, for the clinic's general charitable purposes.

2.   The Richmond County YMCA, Richmond County, Virginia, tax ID #01-23457, to be added the YMCA's building fund.

If any charitable beneficiary named above is not in existence at my death, the Executor shall distribute the share to such other charity or charities my Executor selects that, in his or her sole discretion, most closely satisfy my original charitable intent.

Residue: To Individuals and Charities by Percentages

Residue of Estate. After payment of my debts and estate administration expenses as provided herein, I give the residue of my real and personal property ("my residuary estate") as follows:

1.   Thirty percent (30%) of my residuary estate shall be distributed to my friend, SCOTT P. SMITH, if he survives me, and if he does not, his share shall lapse;

2.   Twenty percent (20%) of my residuary estate shall be distributed to my niece, HELEN P. SAMPLE, if she survives me, and if she does not, her share shall lapse;

3.   Fifteen percent (15%) of my residuary estate shall be distributed to my great-niece, LYNN P. SAMPLE, if she survives me, and if she does not, her share shall lapse;

4.   Thirty-five percent (35%) of my residuary estate shall be distributed to my great-niece, ISABELL D. SAMPLE, if she survives me, and if she does not, her share shall lapse.

If any beneficiary for whom a share is created in paragraphs 1–4 above does not survive me, my Executor shall distribute that beneficiary's share among the beneficiaries who do survive me, pro rata, based on the relative percentages established for each beneficiary who so takes.

Chapter 8

Planning for Minors or Other Young Beneficiaries

Clients with minor children have unique estate-planning issues to consider. The most important is who should serve as guardian of the children while they are minors. The naming of guardians is typically done through the will. Note that a parent is considered the "natural" guardian of a child, so in situations where spouses have divorced, the child will almost always be placed with a surviving parent over any guardian named in a will. The guardian makes the day-to-day decisions for the children that the parents otherwise would have made if alive—that is, where the children live, go to school, and so on. If you name an individual as a guardian, you should consider naming a successor guardian in case the named guardian fails to serve or ceases to serve.

In addition to addressing guardians, the will should address how the assets will be distributed to the minor or young children. There are several options in this respect. Every state, except South Carolina, has adopted some form of the Uniform Transfers to Minors Act (often called the UTMA), which allows a person to appoint a "custodian" in the will to receive assets on behalf of a minor child. The custodian generally has broad authority under the act to use the funds to or for the benefit of the minor. The "to or for the benefit" language means that the custodial account can be paid directly to the beneficiary, or the custodian can pay directly to a provider on behalf of the beneficiary (bypassing the beneficiary). For example, if a custodian is using the account for a beneficiary who is in college, the custodian can make payments directly to the college on behalf of the beneficiary (i.e., rather than writing a large check to the beneficiary and hoping he or she uses the money to pay educational costs). The custodial account will last until the account is fully expended or terminates by its terms once the beneficiary reaches the appropriate age.

I think the custodial approach can be an excellent, low-cost solution for managing assets for a minor beneficiary. Some states allow a custodial account to be held well past age eighteen. For example, Virginia allows a person to create a custodial account lasting until the young person reaches age twenty-one. Some states have extended the twenty-one-year-old limitation to age twenty-five. See appendix 4 for the age limitations for the various state Uniform Transfers to Minors Acts.

Creating a Trust. If you are concerned that age eighteen, twenty-one, or twenty-five (depending on your state's version of the UTMA) is too young for a beneficiary to inherit assets, another approach is to create a trust for the benefit of a beneficiary. The trust is a more formal approach and has some advantages and disadvantages when compared to a custodial account. One advantage is that a trust can manage and marshal the assets for a beneficiary beyond age twenty-one or twenty-five. If you want to create a trust for a beneficiary, you should meet with an attorney because there are a number of issues you will need to discuss in creating it.

Will: Naming Co-Guardians

Guardians. If my spouse does not survive me, I name ROBERT L. SAMPLE and ELLEN P. SAMPLE to have custody and serve as guardians of

the person of each minor child of mine.
I request that no surety be required on
the bond of any guardian so appointed.

Will: Naming Single Guardian, with Successor Guardian

Guardian. If my spouse does not
survive me, I name ROBERT L.
SAMPLE to have custody and serve as
guardian of the person of each minor
child of mine. If ROBERT L. SAMPLE
is unable to serve as guardian or ceases
to serve as guardian for any reason,
I name ELLEN P. SAMPLE to have
custody and serve as guardian of the
person of each minor child of mine. I
request that no surety be required on
the bond of any guardian so appointed.

Will: Custodial Accounts, Age of Majority

Custodial Accounts. My Executor
may distribute any interest vesting
in a minor beneficiary to a custodian
under my state's Uniform Transfers to
Minors Act, as selected by my Executor.

Will: Custodial Account, Extended Age

Custodial Accounts. My Executor
may distribute any interest vesting
in a minor beneficiary to a custodian
under my state's Uniform Transfers to

Minors Act (21 or 25)* as selected by the Executor.

*See appendix 4 for the states that allow custodial accounts to age twenty-one or twenty-five.

Chapter 9

Naming the Executor

Every will should appoint an executor. An executor is the person who is named to gather and manage the estate assets, pay the decedent's debts and administration expenses, and make the required distributions of the estate assets to the beneficiaries. There are several other terms that are similar to or used in place of "executor," including "personal representative" (used in many state statutes), "administrator" (usually the person in charge of an estate where there is not a will), and "executrix" (old-fashioned way of denoting a female executor). I use the term "executor" because it is the most commonly used.

In most states, any individual, bank, or trust company can serve as executor. For the purposes of this book, I am assuming that you will be selecting an individual to serve as executor. Banks and trust companies can be excellent choices in larger, more complicated estates, but they typically have high minimum fees for serving as executor. If you feel that your estate will have complexities that would justify naming a bank or trust company as executor, then you should meet with an attorney to discuss your planning and interview potential executors. Although the estate planning described in this book is simple, the duties of an executor can be complicated. Fortunately, there are professionals (lawyers, accountants, and paralegals) who make a living assisting individual executors with these duties and responsibilities. Also, there are several very good books that new executors can use to help them fulfill their duties. If you do not have a family member or friend who is willing to serve as executor, then I would speak with an attorney in your state about other options available to you. If you do have a family member or friend who would be appropriate, then I recommend that you ask that person whether he or she would be willing to serve before naming that person.

Some states require potential executors to answer questions before they are allowed to serve. For example, in my home state of Virginia, a potential executor must answer the following questions (asked by the clerk of courts) before being granted authority to serve:

Are you a person under a disability?
Have you ever been convicted of a felony?
Have you ever filed for bankruptcy?
Are you now, or have you ever been, an attorney at law in Virginia or elsewhere?

Answering yes to any of these questions will require the individual to provide the clerk or court with additional information before being appointed as executor.

Another consideration in naming an executor is selecting an in-state executor versus an out-of-state executor (sometimes called a "foreign" executor). Most states allow the person creating the will to waive the bond or surety of a named executor. Having a bond, or surety, usually requires an insurance company to issue an insurance policy on the executor's service, ensuring that there will be a source of money should there be a claim against the executor. This type of bond can be very expensive, and its cost is based on the amount of assets in estate and the executor's creditworthiness. As discussed earlier in this book, most clients decide to waive the bond and/or surety for the named executor(s). However, if there is not at least one in-state executor, the court may require a bond or surety, even where it was waived in the will. So whenever practical, naming an in-state executor generally makes the estate administration simpler.

Serving as executor can be a time-consuming endeavor. Most states allow "reasonable compensation" to be paid from the estate to the executor. That amount is typically determined or approved by the court. Some states have adopted a schedule of fees that are deemed reasonable. In either case, executor compensation is typically set as some percentage of the total estate value (e.g., 4 percent of the first $1 million, 3 percent of assets over $1 million). Note that an executor is not required to take compensation if he or she does not want it. If the children are serving as executors of their parents' estate and inherit all of the estate assets, there is generally no benefit to their taking compensation as executors. In fact, if an executor takes compensation, that compensation is taxed as ordinary income, whereas the estate assets are usually received income tax–free. Occasionally, clients name one of several children to act as executor and state that the child so serving shall serve without compensation. Of course, the child could always decline to serve rather than serve without compensation. Knowing how much time and effort it takes to serve as executor, I do not suggest including any language that limits or prohibits compensation.

In the following paragraphs, I have named a primary executor and then a successor executor, to serve in case the primary executor cannot. I have also added a sentence allowing the named executor to nominate another executor to serve with him or her. This is done specifically to address the situation where the person you name is not living in-state and where he or she determines that it would be advantageous to name an in-state executor to serve with him or her. Of the states that allow holographic wills, I am aware of only one, Oklahoma, that will not let an executor appoint a coexecutor. So for most wills, I believe that this provision can be advantageous.

Will: Executor and Successor Executor

> Executor. I name JOHN S. SAMPLE to be my Executor. If JOHN S. SAMPLE fails or ceases to serve as my Executor,

I name HELEN S. SAMPLE to serve as my successor Executor. My Executor may name an additional Executor to serve with my named Executor. I request that no surety be required on the bond of any Executor named by me or any additional Executor named by my Executor.

Will: Coexecutors

Executors. I name SUSAN L. SAMPLE and RANDOLPH D. SAMPLE to serve jointly as my Coexecutors. If either SUSAN L. SAMPLE or RANDOLPH D. SAMPLE fails to serve or ceases to serve as my Executor for any reason, the other of them may continue to serve as my Executor. Either or both of my Executors may name an additional Executor to serve with my Executor. I request that no surety be required on the bond of any Executor named by me or any additional Executor named by my Executor.

Debts and Expenses. One of the executor's primary duties will be to pay the decedent's debts, taxes, and funeral, burial, and estate administration expenses. I typically include a paragraph addressing the costs of delivering tangible personal property to the beneficiaries. If you want the estate to pay the cost of shipping the tangibles to the beneficiaries, it is very important that this language be included in the will. Delivery costs may not appear to be that important, but if you have a grand piano that must be shipped across the country, those expenses suddenly become a big deal.

I also include language addressing joint spousal debts. Generally, an executor must pay all the decedent's debts after death. So when a person who is married dies, the executor has a duty to pay the decedent's debts (including debts joint with the spouse) and then collect contribution from the surviving spouse for one-half the debt (i.e., the surviving spouse technically owes half of all joint debts and must pay the estate back for any debt paid on his or her behalf). In most cases, the surviving spouse is also receiving all of the estate assets. In that case, the executor would be collecting payment from the surviving spouse, only to give that money right back to the surviving spouse as beneficiary. The following language (where "TPP" stands for "tangible personal property") just bypasses this circle of payment and allows the estate to pay all the joint debts without contribution from the spouse.

Will: Married, General Provision to Pay Debts, Estate Pays Cost of TPP Delivery

> Debts and Administration Expenses. My Executor shall pay or arrange for the payment of my legally enforceable debts, my charitable pledges, and the expenses of my funeral, burial, or cremation. My Executor shall not seek contribution from my spouse toward the payment of our joint debts. My Executor shall pay the expenses of delivering my tangible personal property, including transportation, storage, and insurance, as a cost of administering my estate.

Will: Married, General Provision to Pay Debts, Beneficiaries Pay Cost of TPP Delivery

Debts and Administration Expenses. My Executor shall pay or arrange for the payment of my legally enforceable debts, my charitable pledges, and the expenses of my funeral, burial, or cremation. My Executor shall not seek contribution from my spouse toward the payment of our joint debts. Each recipient of tangible personal property shall arrange for delivery of his or her tangible personal property, and each person shall be responsible for the costs of transportation, storage, or insurance.

Will: Single/Widowed/Divorced, General Provision to Pay Debts, Beneficiaries Pay Cost of TPP Delivery

Debts and Administration Expenses. My Executor shall pay or arrange for the payment of my legally enforceable debts, my charitable pledges, and the expenses of my funeral, burial, or cremation. Each recipient of tangible personal property shall arrange for delivery of his or her tangible personal property, and each person shall be responsible for the costs of transportation, storage, or insurance.

Will: Single/Widowed/Divorced, General Provision to Pay Debts, Estate Pays Cost of TPP Delivery

Debts and Administration Expenses. My Executor shall pay or arrange for the payment of my legally enforceable debts, my charitable pledges, and the expenses of my funeral, burial, or cremation. My Executor shall pay the expenses of delivering my tangible personal property, including transportation, storage, and insurance, as a cost of administering my estate.

Chapter 10

Executor Powers

In order to act, the executor must be given certain powers over the estate assets. In most states, the executor automatically has certain powers. In those states, the executor generally has the same power over the property as the deceased owner had during life. Also in those states, the executor has the power to deal with the estate assets but also has a duty to distribute assets to the beneficiaries.

Regardless of your state of residence, I generally recommend including some specific powers in the will in case the will is recorded in a state that requires the powers to be spelled out. These powers include (1) a broad general power to deal with the estate assets (e.g., to sell real estate if necessary); (2) the power to grant a security interest in property if it is necessary for the estate to borrow money; (3) the power to deal with creditors of and to the estate; (4) the power to distribute assets in cash or in kind and in non–pro rata shares; and (5) the power to access and distribute digital assets.

In a minority of states, the executor must be granted specific powers in the will. This can be accomplished in one of two ways. One way is to write out each of the powers the executor should have. The other way is to reference the state statute that lists the powers and indicate in the will that such powers are being "incorporated." Of the states allowing holographic wills, only Virginia (see appendix 5) and West

Virginia (see appendix 6) require the executor's powers to be stated or incorporated by reference in the will.

Executor Powers: All States (Except Virginia and West Virginia)

Executor Powers. My Executor shall have all the powers granted by the law of my state of residence. In addition, I grant my Executor the powers set forth below:

1.   My Executor may sell, exchange, lease, or encumber any assets of my estate upon such terms as my Executor may deem appropriate.

2.   My Executor may grant security interests and execute mortgages, deeds of trust, and other instruments creating security interests upon such terms as my Executor may deem appropriate.

3.   My Executor may compromise and adjust any claims against or on behalf of my estate upon such terms as my Executor may deem appropriate.

4.   My Executor may make distributions to beneficiaries in cash or in specific property, or partly in each, and without making pro rata distributions of specific property.

5. My Executor shall have the right to ascertain value of, access, distribute, and dispose of my digital assets.

Executor Powers: Virginia

Executor Powers. In addition to the powers granted by law, I grant my Executor the powers set forth in Section 64.1-57 of the Code of Virginia in effect on the date of this will. In addition, I grant my Executor the powers set forth below:

1. My Executor may sell, exchange, lease, or encumber any assets of my estate upon such terms as my Executor may deem appropriate.

2. My Executor may grant security interests and execute mortgages, deeds of trust, and other instruments creating security interests upon such terms as my Executor may deem appropriate.

3. My Executor may compromise and adjust any claims against or on behalf of my estate upon such terms as my Executor may deem appropriate.

4.   My Executor may make distributions to beneficiaries in cash or in specific property, or partly in each, and without making pro rata distributions of specific property.

5.   My Executor shall have the right to ascertain value of, access, distribute, and dispose of my digital assets.

Executor Powers: West Virginia

Executor Powers. In addition to the powers granted by law, I grant my Executor the powers set forth in Section 44-5A-3 of the Code of West Virginia in effect on the date of this will. In addition, I grant my Executor the powers set forth below:

1.   My Executor may sell, exchange, lease, or encumber any assets of my estate upon such terms as my Executor may deem appropriate.

2.   My Executor may grant security interests and execute mortgages, deeds of trust, and other instruments creating security interests upon such terms as my Executor may deem appropriate.

3.   My Executor may compromise and adjust any claims against or on behalf of my estate upon such terms as my Executor may deem appropriate.

4.   My Executor may make distributions to beneficiaries in cash or in specific property, or partly in each, and without making pro rata distributions of specific property.

5.   My Executor shall have the right to ascertain value of, access, distribute, and dispose of my digital assets.

Chapter 11

Miscellaneous Provisions

There are a few miscellaneous provisions that are typically addressed in a will. I will go through each of these provisions, including any optional provisions you might consider for inclusion in your will.

Adoption

You should consider whether you want an adopted child or grandchild to inherit as if naturally born to you. Many states have laws that provide that adopted children and grandchildren do not take unless the will explicitly mandates it.

I have included a specific provision addressing anyone adopted after age eighteen. There is an interesting story behind this. In some states, a person can adopt an adult as his or her own "child." A few years ago, a very wealthy couple in Florida divorced and set up a trust for their two biological children. The husband later decided to adopt his girlfriend (in her forties) so that his new, adopted "child" could benefit from the trust set up for the children. This caused quite a stir in the estate planning world. To avoid circumstances like that, I include a provision limiting the definition of adopted children to those who were adopted before age eighteen.

Will: Adoption, Adopted Persons Inherit

> Adoption. Persons related by or through adoption shall take in the same manner as persons related by or through birth except that each person adopted after age eighteen shall not take.

Will: Adoption, Adopted Persons Do Not Inherit

Adoption. Persons related by or through adoption shall not take in the same manner as persons related by or through birth.

Survivorship

Occasionally, you hear a tragic story of a couple who die together in a car accident. Often in such circumstances, it is impossible to determine which spouse died first. The order of death often affects who inherits under each spouse's will. To address this issue, most states have adopted some form of the Uniform Simultaneous Death Act. The fundamental rule is simple. If it cannot be proved that one individual survived the other by 120 hours, that individual is deemed to have predeceased the person who created the will. I typically provide a short paragraph addressing survivorship and often incorporate the 120-hour requirement. In many states, this would be the law even absent this provision, but it is good to have it as a reminder to the executor.

Will: Survivorship, Each Beneficiary Must Survive 120 Hours

Survivorship. A beneficiary shall be deemed to have survived me only if the beneficiary survives me by 120 hours.

Chapter 12

Special Situations—Estate Planning for Pets, Firearms, and Digital Assets

Planning for Pets

In the United States, it is estimated that more than seventy million households own at least one pet (approximately 60 percent of all households). If you want to provide for your pets after death, there are various options, three of which I have used over the years.

Statutory Pet Trust. This type of trust is authorized in forty-six states and allows a client to create an enforceable, long-term plan of care for the pet. These trusts may be appropriate where the amount to be held is significant (e.g., $100,000) and the pet is expected to live a long time (e.g., a horse can easily live into its thirties). State laws typically dictate that at the death of the animal(s), any remaining assets pass as dictated in the decedent's will or trust agreement. These types of trust are complex and should be drafted by an estate planning lawyer.

Transfer to Life-Care Center. These facilities are in various parts of the United States and tend to be a good choice for hard-to-place animals (exotic animals, certain farm animals, and so on). However, these facilities generally require a significant "endowment" or upfront payment. Also, there will be expenses incurred in the actual transfer of the animal to the center (depending on your geographic proximity to the center). This arrangement would need to be worked out during your lifetime and the appropriate paperwork completed prior to your death.

Outright Gift of the Pet and Money. The most popular approach my clients take when providing for pets is to leave an outright bequest of money along with the pet, with the understanding that the beneficiary will use the money to care for the pet for its remaining lifetime. The advantage to this type of planning is that it is a simple and cost-effective way to address pet care. For example, if I wanted my friend to take care of my dogs and I decided $5,000 was the amount I would leave him to do that, I would use the following language.

> Distribution of Pets. If one or more of my dogs survives me, I give my dogs to RICHARD D. SAMPLE, along with the sum of Five Thousand Dollars ($5,000), which I intend to be expended for lifetime care of the dogs. If RICHARD D. SAMPLE is unable or unwilling to take possession of the dogs, I give such dogs and the sum of Five Thousand Dollars ($5,000) to that person my Executor determines will provide a good home for such animals' remaining lifetimes. This gift shall lapse if I have no dog living at the time of my death. I do not intend for this bequest to impose a trust upon any person receiving such dogs and funds.

Firearms as Tangible Personal Property

Firearms may be the most regulated item of tangible personal property in the country. You do not want your firearms to cause your executor or beneficiaries unneeded legal hassles. There are numerous persons under federal and state law who are not able to possess a firearm (called "prohibited persons"). Some examples of prohibited persons include the following:

Anyone who is charged with or has been convicted of a crime that carries more than a one-year jail or prison sentence.

A person who is an unlawful user of, or is addicted to, any controlled substance.

A person who is an illegal alien.

A person who has ever been adjudicated as incompetent.

A person who is under a court order restraining harassment or stalking.

A person who has ever been dishonorably discharged from the armed forces.

A person who has renounced his or her US citizenship.

A person who has ever been convicted of a misdemeanor crime of domestic violence.

It is a crime for an executor to transfer a firearm to a prohibited person. So it is vitally important for you to know whether an intended beneficiary of a firearm is an eligible person to inherit one. One safeguard an executor can follow is to have the firearm delivered to a local federally licensed firearms dealer, who can then transfer the firearm to the intended beneficiary (usually through another federal licensed firearms dealer where the beneficiary lives). Although there will be costs associated with this type of transfer, the executor will not be personally liable if the beneficiary of the firearm turns out to be an ineligible person.

During your life, you should inventory the firearms and accessories that you own. Your inventory should list each gun by make and model, caliber, serial number, and purchase price and date. Having this information will help your executor value the firearms. You may also want to get to know a local federal firearms dealer who can help your executor with the transfer of the firearms at your death.

Digital Assets

There is a relatively new type of property called "digital assets" that is becoming more relevant for clients doing estate planning. These are assets such as bitcoins, phone apps, MP3 songs, and emails. Although such assets are technically a category of intangible personal property, only a few states have updated their statutes to grant the executor the power to collect, value, and distribute these types of assets. It is not sufficient to just give someone your online account password or code for use at death. In fact, the use of a decedent's password or code is often a violation of terms and conditions governing the account and, in certain circumstances, could be a violation of the law.

Note that some airlines allow for the transfer of miles at death— but it is not automatic, and there can be time limitations and fees for getting the miles transferred. Typically, this is done via a transfer form, and if the will clearly identifies the airline and account, it can make such transfers easier to complete. Hotel points and credit card points are less likely to be eligible for transfer, but it does not hurt to ask nicely. For an excellent online article that explains the exact rules for various airlines, hotels, and credit cards, see "What Happens to Your Miles When You Die" by Tiffany Funk at http://onemileatatime. boardingarea.com/author/tiffany/.

Chapter 13

Bringing It All Together

Having gone through the various provisions of a will, I think it will be helpful to see how a complete will might read in some of the more common planning scenarios.

Sample Will: Tangible List, Spouse, Adult Children

Last Will and Testament

of

Sam P. Sample

I, Sam P. Sample, of City, State, on this __ day of
_____ 2017, being of sound mind, do hereby
make this my Last Will and Testament. I revoke
all other wills and codicils I have previously
made. I am married to PATRICIA P. SAMPLE
("my spouse"). I have three children, WILLIAM L.
SAMPLE, ANDREW S. SAMPLE, and REBECCA
A. SAMPLE, who are referred to individually as
"my child" and collectively as "my children."

ARTICLE ONE: DISTRIBUTION OF ESTATE

A.   Tangible Personal Property. I may make a
written list expressing how I wish certain items of
my tangible personal property to be distributed.
In such event, I direct that the list be given effect
under the laws of the state of residence at my death.

I give all my remaining tangible personal property
to my spouse, if my spouse survives me. If my
spouse does not survive me, my Executor shall
distribute my remaining tangible personal
property to my children who survive me in as
nearly equal shares as practical, as may be agreed
upon by my children or, in the absence of such an

agreement, as determined by my Executor in his or her sole discretion.

B.   Residuary Estate. After payment of my debts and estate administration expenses, I give the residue of my real and personal estate ("my residuary estate") to my spouse, if my spouse survives me. If my spouse does not survive me, my Executor shall divide my residuary estate into equal shares, one share for each of my children who survives me and one share for each of my children who predeceases me and leaves one or more descendants who survive me. My Executor shall distribute the share created for a living child to that child outright and free of trust. My Executor shall distribute the share created for a deceased child to such child's living descendants, per stirpes.

ARTICLE TWO: PAYMENT OF DEBTS AND EXPENSES

My Executor shall pay or arrange for the payment of my legally enforceable debts, my charitable pledges, and the expenses of my funeral, burial, or cremation. My Executor shall not seek contribution from my spouse toward the payment of our joint debts. My Executor shall pay the expenses of delivering my tangible personal property, including transportation, storage, and insurance, as a cost of administering my estate.

ARTICLE THREE: EXECUTOR PROVISIONS

A.   Executor. I name my spouse to be my Executor ("my Executor"). If my spouse is unable to serve as my Executor or ceases to serve as Executor for any reason, I name REBECCA A. SAMPLE to be my successor Executor. My Executor may, in my Executor's sole discretion, name any individual or any bank or trust company having trust powers to serve with my Executor as a Coexecutor.

B.   Surety and Waiver of Appraisal and Accountings. I direct that no surety shall be required on the bond of any Executor nominated herein or appointed hereunder. I request that an appraisal of my estate be waived.

ARTICLE FOUR: ADMINISTRATION OF ESTATE

A.   Executor Powers. I grant my Executor all the powers granted under the law of the state where I am a resident at my death. In addition, I grant my Executor the powers set forth below:

     1.   My Executor may sell, exchange, lease, or encumber any assets of my estate upon such terms as my Executor may deem appropriate.

     2.   My Executor may grant security interests and execute mortgages, deeds of trust, and other instruments creating

security interests upon such terms as my Executor may deem appropriate.

3.   My Executor may compromise and adjust any claims against or on behalf of my estate upon such terms as my Executor may deem appropriate.

4.   My Executor may make distributions to beneficiaries in cash or in specific property, or partly in each, and without making pro rata distributions of specific property.

5.   My Executor shall have the right to ascertain value of, access, distribute, and dispose of my digital assets.

B.   Custodial Accounts. My Executor shall distribute any interest vesting in a minor beneficiary to a custodian under my state's Uniform Transfers to Minors Act, as selected by my Executor.

ARTICLE FIVE: MISCELLANEOUS PROVISIONS

A.   Adoption. A person related by or through adoption shall take under my Last Will and Testament as if related by or through birth, except that a person adopted after reaching age eighteen and descendants of such person shall not take.

B.   Survivorship. Any beneficiary who fails to survive me by 120 hours shall be deemed to have predeceased me.

I have signed this, my Last Will and Testament, on the ___ day of _____ 2017.

Sam P. Sample

Sample Will: No Tangible List, Spouse, Adult Children

Last Will and Testament
of
Sam P. Sample

I, Sam P. Sample, of City, State, on this __ day of
_____ 2017, being of sound mind, do hereby
make this my Last Will and Testament. I revoke
all other wills and codicils I have previously
made. I am married to PATRICIA P. SAMPLE
("my spouse"). I have three children, WILLIAM L.
SAMPLE, ANDREW S. SAMPLE, and REBECCA
A. SAMPLE, who are referred to individually as
"my child" and collectively as "my children."

ARTICLE ONE: DISTRIBUTION OF ESTATE

A.   Tangible Personal Property. I give all my
tangible personal property to my spouse, if my
spouse survives me. If my spouse does not survive
me, my Executor shall distribute my remaining
tangible personal property to my children who
survive me in as nearly equal shares as practical,
as may be agreed upon by my children or, in the
absence of such an agreement, as determined by
my Executor in his or her sole discretion.

B.   Residuary Estate. After payment of my
debts and estate administration expenses, I give
the residue of my real and personal estate ("my
residuary estate") to my spouse, if my spouse

survives me. If my spouse does not survive me, my Executor shall divide my residuary estate into equal shares, one share for each of my children who survives me and one share for each of my children who predeceases me and leaves one or more descendants who survive me. The Executor shall distribute the share created for a living child to that child outright and free of trust. My Executor shall distribute the share created for a deceased child to such child's living descendants, per stirpes.

ARTICLE TWO: PAYMENT OF DEBTS AND EXPENSES

My Executor shall pay or arrange for the payment of my legally enforceable debts, my charitable pledges, and the expenses of my funeral, burial, or cremation. My Executor shall not seek contribution from my spouse toward the payment of our joint debts. My Executor shall pay the expenses of delivering my tangible personal property, including transportation, storage, and insurance, as a cost of administering my estate.

ARTICLE THREE: EXECUTOR PROVISIONS

A.   Executor. I name my spouse to be my Executor ("my Executor"). If my spouse is unable to serve as my Executor or ceases to serve as Executor for any reason, I name REBECCA A. SAMPLE to be my successor Executor. My Executor may, in my Executor's sole discretion, name any individual or any bank or trust company having trust powers to serve with my Executor as a Coexecutor.

B.   Surety and Waiver of Appraisal and Accountings. I direct that no surety shall be required on the bond of any Executor nominated herein or appointed hereunder. I request that an appraisal of my estate be waived.

ARTICLE FOUR: ADMINISTRATION OF ESTATE

A.   Executor Powers. I grant my Executor all the powers granted under the law of the state where I am a resident at my death. In addition, I grant my Executor the powers set forth below:

1.   My Executor may sell, exchange, lease, or encumber any assets of my estate upon such terms as my Executor may deem appropriate.

2.   My Executor may grant security interests and execute mortgages, deeds of trust, and other instruments creating security interests upon such terms as my Executor may deem appropriate.

3.   My Executor may compromise and adjust any claims against or on behalf of my estate upon such terms as my Executor may deem appropriate.

4. My Executor may make distributions to beneficiaries in cash or in specific property, or partly in each, and without making pro rata distributions of specific property.

5. My Executor shall have the right to ascertain value of, access, distribute, and dispose of my digital assets.

B. Custodial Accounts. My Executor shall distribute any interest vesting in a minor beneficiary to a custodian under my state's Uniform Transfers to Minors Act, as selected by my Executor.

ARTICLE FIVE: MISCELLANEOUS PROVISIONS

A. Adoption. A person related by or through adoption shall take under my Last Will and Testament as if related by or through birth, except that a person adopted after reaching age eighteen and the descendants of such person shall not take.

B. Survivorship. Any beneficiary who fails to survive me by 120 hours shall be deemed to have predeceased me.

I have signed this, my Last Will and Testament, on the __ day of _____ 2017.

Sam P. Sample

Sample Will: Tangible List, Spouse, Minor Children

Last Will and Testament
of
Sam P. Sample

I, Sam P. Sample, of City, State, on this ___ day of ___ 2017, being of sound mind, do hereby make this my Last Will and Testament. I revoke all other wills and codicils I have previously made. I am married to PATRICIA P. SAMPLE ("my spouse"). I have three children, WILLIAM L. SAMPLE, ANDREW S. SAMPLE, and REBECCA A. SAMPLE. These children and any other children born to or adopted by me shall be referred to individually as "my child" and collectively as "my children."

ARTICLE ONE: DISTRIBUTION OF ESTATE

A.   Tangible Personal Property. I may make a written list expressing how I wish certain items of my tangible personal property to be distributed. In such event, I direct that the list be given effect under the laws of the state of my residence at my death.

I give my remaining tangible personal property to my spouse, if my spouse survives me. If my spouse does not survive me, I give my remaining tangible personal property in as nearly equal shares as my Executor deems practical to my children who survive me; it is provided that my Executor may sell any such tangible personal property that my Executor deems inappropriate for distribution in kind and add the net proceeds of sale to my residuary estate.

My Executor may distribute tangible personal property passing to a minor to any adult person with whom a minor resides, and the adult person's receipt shall be a sufficient voucher in the accounts of my Executor.

B.   Residuary Estate. After payment of my debts and estate administration expenses, I give the residue of my real and personal estate ("my residuary estate") to my spouse, if my spouse survives me. If my spouse does not survive me, my Executor shall divide my residuary estate into equal shares, one share for each of my children who survives me and one share for each of my children who predeceases me and leaves one or more descendants who survive me. My Executor shall distribute the share created for a living child to that child outright and free of trust.

ARTICLE TWO: PAYMENT OF DEBTS AND EXPENSES

My Executor shall pay or arrange for the payment of my legally enforceable debts, my charitable pledges, and the expenses of my funeral, burial, or cremation. My Executor shall not seek contribution from my spouse toward the payment of our joint debts. My Executor shall pay the expenses of delivering my tangible personal property, including transportation, storage, and insurance, as a cost of administering my estate.

ARTICLE THREE: EXECUTOR PROVISIONS

A.   Executor. I name my spouse to be my Executor ("my Executor"). If my spouse is unable to serve as my Executor or ceases to serve as Executor for any reason, I name REBECCA A. SAMPLE to be my successor Executor. My Executor may, in my Executor's sole discretion, name any individual or any bank or trust company having trust powers to serve with my Executor as a Coexecutor.

B.   Surety and Waiver of Appraisal and Accountings. I direct that no surety shall be required on the bond of any Executor nominated herein or appointed hereunder. I request that an appraisal of my estate be waived.

ARTICLE FOUR: ADMINISTRATION OF ESTATE

A.   Executor Powers. I grant my Executor all the powers granted under the law of the state where I am a resident at my death. In addition, I grant my Executor the powers set forth below:

1.   My Executor may sell, exchange, lease, or encumber any assets of my estate

upon such terms as my Executor may deem appropriate.

2.   My Executor may grant security interests and execute mortgages, deeds of trust, and other instruments creating security interests upon such terms as my Executor may deem appropriate.

3.   My Executor may compromise and adjust any claims against or on behalf of my estate upon such terms as my Executor may deem appropriate.

4.   My Executor may make distributions to beneficiaries in cash or in specific property, or partly in each, and without making pro rata distributions of specific property.

5.   My Executor shall have the right to ascertain value of, access, distribute, and dispose of my digital assets.

B.   Custodial Accounts. My Executor shall distribute any interest vesting in a minor beneficiary to a custodian under my state's Uniform Transfers to Minors Act, as selected by my Executor.

ARTICLE FIVE: MISCELLANEOUS PROVISIONS

A.   Adoption. A person related by or through adoption shall take under my Last Will and Testament as if related by or through birth, except that a person adopted after reaching age eighteen and the descendants of such person shall not so take.

B.   Survivorship. Any beneficiary who fails to survive me by 120 hours shall be deemed to have predeceased me.

C.   Guardians. If my spouse does not survive me, I name ROBERT L. SAMPLE and ELLEN P. SAMPLE to have custody and serve as guardians of the person of each minor child of mine. I request that no surety be required on the bond of any guardian so appointed.

I have signed this, my Last Will and Testament, on the ___ day of _____ 2017.

Sam P. Sample

Sample Will: Tangible List, Single/Widowed/Divorced, Specific Bequests, No Children, Residue to Various Beneficiaries.

Last Will and Testament
of
Sam P. Sample

I, Sam P. Sample, of City, State, on this ___ day of _____ 2017, being of sound mind, do hereby make this my Last Will and Testament. I revoke all other wills and codicils I have previously made. I am single, and I have no children.

ARTICLE ONE: DISTRIBUTION OF ESTATE

A.　　Tangible Personal Property. I may make a written list expressing how I wish certain items of my tangible personal property to be distributed. In such event, I direct that the list be given effect under the laws of my state of residence at my death. I direct that my Executor sell my remaining tangible personal property not distributed by my list and add the net proceeds of sale to my residuary estate, to be distributed as provided in paragraph D below.

My Executor may distribute tangible personal property passing to a minor to any adult person with whom a minor resides, and that adult person's receipt shall be a sufficient voucher in the accounts of my Executor.

B.   Specific Bequests.

1.   I give and bequeath the sum of Five Thousand Dollars ($5,000) to the Community Foundation, 123 Elm Street, Richmond, Virginia, tax ID #12-34567, for use in the foundation's general charitable purposes.

2.   I give the sum of Ten Thousand Dollars ($10,000) to the Sample School of Professional and Continuing Studies, 445 Oak Street, Richmond, Virginia, tax ID #23-456787, for use in the school's general charitable purposes.

If any charitable beneficiary named above is not in existence at my death, my Executor shall distribute the bequest to such other charity or charities my Executor shall select that, in the sole discretion of my Executor, most closely satisfy my original charitable intent.

C.   Personal Residence. I direct that my Executor sell my personal residence, currently located at 123 Main Street, Richmond, Virginia, and add net proceeds of sale to my residuary estate, to be distributed as provided in paragraph D below.

D.   Residue of Estate. After payment of my debts and estate administration expenses as provided herein, I give the residue of my real and personal property ("my residuary estate") as follows:

1.   Thirty percent (30%) of my residuary estate shall be distributed to my friend, SCOTT P. SMITH, if he survives me, and if he does not, his share shall lapse;

2.   Twenty percent (20%) of my residuary estate shall be distributed to my niece, HELEN P. SAMPLE, if she survives me, and if she does not, her share shall lapse;

3.   Fifteen percent (15%) of my residuary estate shall be distributed to my great-niece, LYNN P. SAMPLE, if she survives me, and if she does not, her share shall lapse;

4.   Thirty-five percent (35%) of my residuary estate shall be distributed to my great-niece, ISABELL D. SAMPLE, if she survives me, and if she does not, her share shall lapse.

If any beneficiary for whom a share is created in paragraphs 1–4 above does not survive me, my Executor shall distribute that beneficiary's share among the surviving beneficiaries, pro rata, based on the relative percentages established for each beneficiary who so takes.

ARTICLE TWO: PAYMENT OF DEBTS AND EXPENSES

My Executor shall pay or arrange for the payment of my legally enforceable debts, my charitable pledges, and the expenses of my funeral, burial, or cremation. My Executor shall pay the expenses of delivering my tangible personal property, including transportation, storage, and insurance, as a cost of administering my estate.

ARTICLE THREE: EXECUTOR PROVISIONS

A.   Executor. I name my nephew, JOSEPH H. SAMPLE, to be my Executor ("my Executor"). If JOSEPH H. SAMPLE is unable to serve as my Executor or ceases to serve as Executor for any reason, I name SANDRA S. SAMPLE to be my successor Executor. My Executor may, in my Executor's sole discretion, name any individual or any bank or trust company having trust powers to serve with my Executor as a Coexecutor.

B.   Surety and Waiver of Appraisal and Accountings. I direct that no surety shall be required on the bond of any Executor nominated herein or appointed hereunder. I request that an appraisal of my estate be waived.

ARTICLE FOUR: ADMINISTRATION OF ESTATE

A.   Executor Powers. I grant my Executor all the powers granted under the law of the state where I am a resident at my death. In addition, I grant my Executor the powers set forth below:

     1.   My Executor may sell, exchange, lease, or encumber any assets of my estate upon such terms as my Executor may deem appropriate.

     2.   My Executor may grant security interests and execute mortgages, deeds of trust, and other instruments creating security interests upon such terms as my Executor may deem appropriate.

     3.   My Executor may compromise and adjust any claims against or on behalf of my estate upon such terms as my Executor may deem appropriate.

     4.   My Executor may make distributions to beneficiaries in cash or in specific property, or partly in each, and without making pro rata distributions of specific property. Assets allocated to one share may be of different character or have different income-tax bases than assets allocated to another share.

5.   My Executor shall have the right to ascertain value of, access, distribute, and dispose of my digital assets.

B.   Custodial Accounts. My Executor shall distribute any interest vesting in a minor beneficiary to a custodian under my state's Uniform Transfers to Minors Act, as selected by my Executor.

ARTICLE FIVE: MISCELLANEOUS PROVISIONS

A.   Adoption. A person related by or through adoption shall take under my Last Will and Testament as if related by or through birth, except that a person adopted after reaching age eighteen and the descendants of such person shall not take.

B.   Survivorship. Any beneficiary who fails to survive me by 120 hours shall be deemed to have predeceased me.

I have signed and sealed my will this __ day of _____ 2017.

Sam P. Sample

Sample Will: Single/Widowed/Divorced, Tangible List, Specific Bequests, Residence Sold, Residue to Charity

Last Will and Testament
of
Sam P. Sample

I, Sam P. Sample, of City, State, on this ___ day of _____ 2017, being of sound mind, do hereby make this my Last Will and Testament. I revoke all other wills and codicils I have previously made. I am single, and I have no children.

ARTICLE ONE: DISTRIBUTION OF ESTATE

A.   Tangible Personal Property. I may make a written list expressing how I wish certain items of my tangible personal property to be distributed. In such event, I direct that the list be given effect under the laws of the state of my residence at my death. I direct that my Executor sell my remaining tangible personal property not distributed by my list and add the net proceeds of sale to my residuary estate, to be distributed as provided in paragraph D below.

B.   Specific Bequests.

    1.   I give and bequeath the sum of Five Thousand Dollars ($5,000) to my niece, SANDRA S. SAMPLE, if she survives me, and if she does not, this gift shall lapse.

2.   I give the sum of Ten Thousand Dollars ($10,000) to my nephew, JOSEPH H. SAMPLE, if he survives me, and if he does not, this gift shall lapse.

C.   Personal Residence. I direct that my Executor sell my personal residence, currently located at 123 Main Street, Richmond, Virginia, and add net proceeds of sale to my residuary estate, to be distributed as provided in paragraph D below.

D.   Residuary Estate. After payment of my debts and estate administration expenses as provided herein, I direct my Executor to divide and distribute the residue of my real and personal property ("my residuary estate") as follows:

1.   Fifty percent (50%) of my residuary estate shall be distributed to the Community Foundation, 123 Elm Street, Richmond, Virginia, tax ID #12-34567, for use in the foundation's general charitable purposes; and

2.   Fifty percent (50%) of my residuary estate shall be distributed to the Sample School of Professional and Continuing Studies, 445 Oak Street, Richmond, Virginia, tax ID #23-456787, for use in the school's general charitable purposes.

If any charitable beneficiary named above is not in existence at my death, the Executor shall distribute the bequest to such other charity or charities my Executor shall select that, in the sole discretion of my Executor, most closely satisfy my original charitable intent.

ARTICLE TWO: PAYMENT OF DEBTS AND EXPENSES

My Executor shall pay or arrange for the payment of my legally enforceable debts, my charitable pledges, and the expenses of my funeral, burial, or cremation. My Executor shall pay the expenses of delivering my tangible personal property, including transportation, storage, and insurance, as a cost of administering my estate.

ARTICLE THREE: EXECUTOR PROVISIONS

A.   Executor. I name my nephew, JOSEPH H. SAMPLE, to be my Executor ("my Executor"). If JOSEPH H. SAMPLE is unable to serve as my Executor or ceases to serve as Executor for any reason, I name SANDRA S. SAMPLE to be my successor Executor. My Executor may, in my Executor's sole discretion, name any individual or any bank or trust company having trust powers to serve with my Executor as a Coexecutor.

B.   Surety and Waiver of Appraisal and Accountings. I direct that no surety shall be required on the bond of any Executor nominated herein or appointed hereunder. I request that an appraisal of my estate be waived.

ARTICLE FOUR: ADMINISTRATION OF ESTATE

A.   Executor Powers. I grant my Executor all the powers granted under the law of the state where I am a resident at my death. In addition, I grant my Executor the powers set forth below:

1.   My Executor may sell, exchange, lease, or encumber any assets of my estate upon such terms as my Executor may deem appropriate.

2.   My Executor may grant security interests and execute mortgages, deeds of trust, and other instruments creating security interests upon such terms as my Executor may deem appropriate.

3.   My Executor may compromise and adjust any claims against or on behalf of my estate upon such terms as my Executor may deem appropriate.

4.   My Executor may make distributions to beneficiaries in cash or in specific property, or partly in each, and without making pro rata distributions of specific property. Assets allocated to one share may be of different

character or have different income-tax bases than assets allocated to another share.

5.   My Executor shall have the right to ascertain value of, access, distribute, and dispose of my digital assets.

B.   Custodial Accounts. My Executor shall distribute any interest vesting in a minor beneficiary to a custodian under my state's Uniform Transfers to Minors Act, as selected by my Executor.

ARTICLE FIVE: MISCELLANEOUS PROVISIONS

A.   Adoption. A person related by or through adoption shall take under my Last Will and Testament as if related by or through birth, except that a person adopted after reaching age eighteen and the descendants of such person shall not take.

B.   Survivorship. Any beneficiary who fails to survive me by 120 hours shall be deemed to have predeceased me.

I have signed and sealed my will this ___ day of _____ 2017.

Sam P. Sample

Sample Will: Single/Widowed/Divorced, Tangible List, Residence Sold, Residue to Siblings or Nieces and Nephews

Last Will and Testament

of

Sam P. Sample

I, Sam P. Sample, of City, State, on this ___ day of _____ 2017, being of sound mind, do hereby make this my Last Will and Testament. I revoke all other wills and codicils I have previously made. I am single, and I have no children.

ARTICLE ONE: DISTRIBUTION OF ESTATE

A.   Tangible Personal Property. I may make a list expressing how I wish certain items of my tangible personal property to be distributed. In such event, I direct that the list be given effect under the laws of the state of my residence at my death. I direct that my Executor sell my remaining tangible personal property not distributed by my list and add the net proceeds of sale to my residuary estate, to be distributed as provided in paragraph D below.

B.   Specific Bequests.

   1.   I give and bequeath the sum of Five Thousand Dollars ($5,000) to my friend, SANDRA S. SAMPLE, if she survives me, and if she does not, this gift shall lapse.

2.   I give the sum of Ten Thousand Dollars ($10,000) to my friend, FRANK H. SMITH, if he survives me, and if he does not, this gift shall lapse.

C.   Personal Residence. I direct that my Executor sell my personal residence, currently located at 123 Main Street, Richmond, Virginia, and add net proceeds of sale to my residuary estate, to be distributed as provided in paragraph D below.

D.   Residuary Estate. After payment of my debts and estate administration expenses as provided herein, I direct my Executor to divide and distribute the residue of my real and personal property ("my residuary estate") into equal shares, one share for each of my siblings who survives me and one share for each of my siblings who predeceases me and leaves one or more descendants who survive me. The Executor shall distribute the share for a living sibling to such sibling, outright and free of trust. My Executor shall distribute the share created for a deceased sibling to such sibling's living descendants, per stirpes.

ARTICLE TWO: PAYMENT OF DEBTS AND EXPENSES

My Executor shall pay or arrange for the payment of my legally enforceable debts, my charitable pledges, and the expenses of my funeral, burial, or cremation. My Executor shall pay the expenses of delivering my tangible personal property, including transportation, storage, and insurance, as a cost of administering my estate.

ARTICLE THREE: EXECUTOR PROVISIONS

A. Executor. I name my nephew, JOSEPH H. SAMPLE, to be my Executor ("my Executor"). If JOSEPH H. SAMPLE is unable to serve as my Executor or ceases to serve as Executor for any reason, I name SANDRA S. SAMPLE to be my successor Executor. My Executor may, in my Executor's sole discretion, name any individual or any bank or trust company having trust powers to serve with my Executor as a Coexecutor.

B. Surety and Waiver of Appraisal and Accountings. I direct that no surety shall be required on the bond of any Executor nominated herein or appointed hereunder. I request that an appraisal of my estate be waived.

ARTICLE FOUR: ADMINISTRATION OF ESTATE

A. Executor Powers. I grant my Executor all the powers granted under the law of the state where I am a resident at my death. In addition, I grant my Executor the powers set forth below:

1. My Executor may sell, exchange, lease, or encumber any assets of my estate

upon such terms as my Executor may deem appropriate.

2.   My Executor may grant security interests and execute mortgages, deeds of trust, and other instruments creating security interests upon such terms as my Executor may deem appropriate.

3.   My Executor may compromise and adjust any claims against or on behalf of my estate upon such terms as my Executor may deem appropriate.

4.   My Executor may make distributions to beneficiaries in cash or in specific property, or partly in each, and without making pro rata distributions of specific property. Assets allocated to one share may be of different character or have different income-tax bases than assets allocated to another share.

5.   My Executor shall have the right to ascertain value of, access, distribute, and dispose of my digital assets.

B.   Custodial Accounts. My Executor shall distribute any interest vesting in a minor beneficiary under my state's Uniform Transfers to Minors Act, as selected by my Executor.

ARTICLE FIVE: MISCELLANEOUS PROVISIONS

A.   Adoption. A person related by or through adoption shall take under my Last Will and Testament as if related by or through birth, except that a person adopted after reaching age eighteen and the descendants of such person shall not take.

B.   Survivorship. Any beneficiary who fails to survive me by 120 hours shall be deemed to have predeceased me.

I have signed and sealed my will this ___ day of _____ 2017.

Sam P. Sample

Checklist for Preparing a Simple Will

Introductory Paragraph

    ✓ Use your full legal name. It is okay to use middle initials, but if you have a common name (e.g., John Smith), a complete middle name is preferable. Include "formerly known as" information if you have assets held in another name (e.g., Jane F. Doe f/k/a Jane Smith).

    ✓ Revoke all prior wills and codicils.

    ✓ Name your children. Determine whether you want to include stepchildren in the definition of children.

Article One: Distribution of Estate

    ✓ Determine whether you want to include specific bequests of tangible personal property and/or prepare a list of items to go to certain beneficiaries.

    ✓ Determine whether you want to make specific bequests of cash.

    ✓ Determine whether you want to make a specific devise of real estate or whether you want your executor to sell the real estate.

    ✓ Determine how you want the remaining assets (the residue) of the estate to pass. Decide how you want the assets to be distributed if a beneficiary predeceases you.

Article Two: Payment of Debts and Expenses

    ✓ Include a paragraph instructing your executor to make payment of your debts and administration expenses.

Article Three: Executor

- ✓ Consider who will serve as executor of the estate. In case that person cannot serve, consider naming a backup.
- ✓ Include language waiving surety on an executor's bond.

Article Four: Administration of the Estate

- ✓ Include the appropriate powers paragraph.
- ✓ Include appropriate language to allow a custodian to be appointed under your state law.

Article Five: Miscellaneous

- ✓ Determine whether you want adopted beneficiaries to take as if they were blood relatives.
- ✓ Consider the appropriate survivorship period for your beneficiaries.
- ✓ Sign and date your will! If you have dated the first and last pages, make sure both dates match.

Make sure to keep your original will in a safe location. Your executor will need to be able to locate the original will in order to record the will at your death. Historically, lawyers have advised clients to store these and other important documents in a safe deposit box. There can be a logistical downside to this approach because the family members may not have immediate access to a safe deposit box after death (assuming, also, they can find the key). If you have a joint owner on the box, that can decrease the likelihood of this becoming as issue. Also, some states have addressed this issue through legislation allowing limited access to such boxes after death. But if someone else cannot access your safe deposit box immediately after your death, I recommend that you keep your original will in a fireproof safe or locked file cabinet. In either event, let the executor know where the original will is located and, if it is in a safe deposit box, where the box key will be located.

I would be remiss if I did not point out the other two documents that make up a core estate plan. In addition to a will, I suggest that you prepare (or have prepared for you) a power of attorney and advance medical directive. A power of attorney is a document created by the "principal" (you) naming an "agent" to act for you with respect to management of your property and financial affairs. A power of attorney is generally written very broadly to permit the agent to do almost anything that you could do yourself. Sometimes you hear the term "durable power of attorney." Here the word "durable" just means that the power of attorney remains effective in the event of your disability or incapacity. Although an agent is acting on your behalf, the agent is acting in a fiduciary capacity—meaning that this person can act only in your best interest. Generally, a power of attorney can be revoked by you at any time while you have capacity and is automatically revoked at your death.

The advance medical directive is a combination of three documents: (1) a "living will," (2) a health care power of attorney, and (3) an anatomical gift authorization. The living will instructs your physician to withhold certain artificial life-support measures if you are in a terminal condition and your death is imminent or if you are in a persistent vegetative state. The health care power of attorney appoints an agent and alternate agent(s) to make other health care decisions on your behalf if you are not competent to make those decisions yourself. If you are not able to act, your agent can make certain medical decisions on your behalf (e.g., decide whether to approve surgery, treatment, nursing care, or hospital admission) but only *in a manner consistent* with your directive in the living will portion of the document. The anatomical gift authorization allows you to make anatomical donations for organ transplant or research upon your death, and you can appoint an agent and alternate agent(s) to implement that authorization.

Although an in-depth review of powers of attorney and advance medical directives is beyond the scope of this book, they are both very important documents that you should consider creating. Because neither document has the complex execution formalities of a will (although the advance medical directive is usually witnessed), these documents can be safely prepared online, and, in fact, some states have free sample forms available for consumer use. For the purposes of the advance medical directive, there is an excellent website created by Everplans that has free, state-specific advance medical directive forms. The site also has some very good information about estate planning and storage of estate planning documents. To view these forms, go to https://www.everplans.com/articles/state-by-state-advance-directive-forms.

Chapter 14

Updating or Changing Your Will

Your will does not become operative until your death. So while you are alive and competent, you can change your will. Typically, this is done through a codicil to your will. For example, if I were replacing paragraph A of Article II in my will to change the amount of a cash bequest to my son, I would prepare a codicil as shown below.

Codicil to Last Will and Testament
of
John H. Sample

I, JOHN H. SAMPLE, of City, State, make this codicil to my Last Will and Testament that was signed on August 5, 2005.

FIRST: I hereby revoke paragraph A of Article II of my Last Will and Testament in its entirety and insert the following paragraph in its place:

A. I give my son, RANDOLPH P. SMITH, the sum of Ten Thousand Dollars ($10,000) if he survives me, and if he does not, this bequest shall lapse.

SECOND: Except as changed by this codicil, I confirm, ratify, and republish my Last Will and Testament.

I have signed and sealed this codicil to my Last Will and Testament on this _____ day of _____ 2017.

John H. Sample

Be careful in identifying what articles or paragraphs you are replacing. I have seen a codicil that was drafted with language to replace a specific paragraph only—but where the draftsman mistakenly replaced the entire article, leaving a large, unintentional gap in the will. If you are handwriting your will, it may be just as easy to rewrite the entire will with your changes rather than creating a codicil.

One event that may call for revisiting and modifying your will is a divorce. In most states, if after making a will, a person is divorced, the divorce revokes any disposition or appointment of property made by the will to the former spouse. Unless the will expressly provides otherwise, any provision nominating the former spouse as executor, trustee, conservator, or guardian is also revoked. Nevertheless, the safer approach is to rewrite your will and address the beneficiary changes and executor provisions, if needed. If, on the other hand, you are divorced and for some reason want to include your ex-spouse in your estate planning, you should clearly indicate in the will that the divorce has occurred and that you are overriding any state law that revokes provisions made for the ex-spouse.

Note that these statutes generally apply only after the divorce is finalized. Therefore, if the divorce proceeding is expected to drag on, you should prepare a new will (or codicil) addressing the changes you want to make now. I have handled more than one estate where the spouses were separated but one spouse died unexpectedly, prior to the finalization of the divorce.

As a reminder, you should also review your designated beneficiary selections on assets such as life insurance, IRAs, and 401(k)s. Divorce may not automatically revoke the ex-spouse's rights in some assets—especially 401k(s) and other federal plans—so be diligent in addressing those matters if divorcing.

Chapter 15

Probate Assets versus Nonprobate Assets

Now that you have the knowledge and guidance to make a valid will, let's talk about the other ways assets can be transferred to your beneficiaries at your death. Your will controls only a certain type of assets, called "probate" assets. Probate assets include anything that you own just in your name alone and any assets that have your estate as the named beneficiary. Other assets are called "nonprobate" assets, and those assets pass independently of your will (i.e., your will does not control the disposition of nonprobate assets). Any assets that have designated beneficiaries or that are titled in a way that they pass directly to a named beneficiary are nonprobate assets. For example, life insurance, individual retirement accounts (IRAs), 401(k)s, and other retirement plans have designated beneficiaries who inherit the assets at death of the account owner. If you have an IRA that names your spouse as the primary beneficiary, at your death that account will pass directly to your spouse, bypassing your will. Life insurance also has designated beneficiaries and passes directly to whom you name as the primary beneficiary. The only times these types of assets pass through your will are (1) if you named your estate as the beneficiary or (2) if no beneficiary was named (or survived you), and the default beneficiary was the estate.

Having your estate named as the primary beneficiary (or dying without naming a beneficiary) is not the most cost-efficient way for these assets to pass to your beneficiaries. When the estate becomes the beneficiary, the assets will be probate assets, and the estate will pay some expenses in the form of probate taxes and administration costs to transfer the assets to the ultimate beneficiaries. Usually, the better estate plan is to name beneficiaries for these types of assets in a manner that mirrors your planning done in your will.

For example, if I wanted to leave all my assets to my spouse if she survived me and to my children if she did not, I would designate my spouse as the primary beneficiary on the designated beneficiary form and would name my children as the secondary or contingent beneficiaries. One thing I would be careful to determine is what happens according to the designated beneficiary form if my spouse predeceases me *and* one of my children predeceases me. Sometimes, the forms mandate that the deceased child's descendants take the share the child would have taken had he or she survived (or the same as *per stirpes*, discussed in detail in chapter 3). Other times, the form mandates that *only* the surviving named children will take (i.e., the deceased child's children are cut out).

Another type of nonprobate asset is jointly owned assets (with survivorship). For example, when a husband and wife own their house jointly, that typically means that at the first spouse's death, the survivor will own the entire house. Also, another type of nonprobate asset is an account that has a transfer on death (TOD) or payable on death (POD) designation. At your death, the TOD (typically security accounts) or POD (typically bank accounts) account will pass directly to whomever you have named as beneficiary.

So to the extent that you can designate nonprobate assets to pass to your intended beneficiaries, that will decrease the number of assets that pass through your will. In fact, in planning for married couples, it is not unusual to see all their assets held in a way that they pass outside the will. That works fine at the first death but does not lessen the importance of the will (especially at the second spouse's death or should the spouses die simultaneous deaths).

Chapter 16

Making Life Easier on Your Loved Ones after You Die

By preparing a will, you have taken a very important step in making life easier on your loved ones at your death. However, there are some other actions that you can take now that will make your passing less stressful on those around you.

In some states, the named executor will need to locate two or more witnesses to confirm that the will was, in fact, written in the person's handwriting. In my experience, witnesses have been neighbors, relatives, friends, coworkers, or priests or ministers—a witness can be basically anyone who is familiar with the person's handwriting. It will be helpful for one or more of these persons to keep holiday cards, letters, notes, or other writing samples.

One issue clients often bring up is what they should do about funeral and burial decisions. Specifically, the clients ask, "Should we include funeral or burial decisions in our will?" My answer is no. By the time someone locates your will and the executor takes the necessary steps to start acting on behalf of your estate, you will be long buried or cremated. Moreover, if you do go to the trouble to spell out what you want done at death, and after your death your family does something different (because they have not read your will yet), there can be significant costs to remedy that. So I do not recommend that you put specific funeral, cremation, or burial instructions in the will.

So the follow-up question is always "Where should we put those instructions?" I developed a form over the years called "What Your Survivors Should Know," and it is included in this book as appendix 7. This form is meant to be a road map for your survivors and to help them navigate difficult decisions at a difficult time. This form starts with a section that gives your family information that will help them in writing an obituary. The form then provides a section in which to lay out funeral, burial, or cremation desires. It includes a place for you to list your advisers and their contact information and finally provides a place for you to list your accounts, assets, and important documents and their locations. Another way to relieve some of the stress of your death is to prepay for the specific funeral and/or cremation services you want. There are some advantages to doing this. One is that you pay for only those services you feel are important (and your grieving family will not be upsold). Second, you can freeze the costs of the funeral now, and if those costs subsequently rise more than the small amount of interest you make on your money, your estate will have saved money on these costs. If you do prepay, I suggest looking at a preneed plan that will move with you if you move. Some funeral homes will guarantee that the costs will not increase even if you die in a locality different from the one you lived in when the plan was put in place (e.g., if you move from Iowa to New York, there will be no additional costs).

Chapter 17

Some Tips on Serving as Executor

When you select an executor to serve under your will, it will be helpful to let them know a little about what to expect. Although the document "What Your Survivors Should Know" has some helpful information for your executor, especially as to where your assets may be located at your death, I am also providing some helpful information addressing some of the main issues I see when individuals serve as executors.

Avoiding Certain Pitfalls in Serving as Executor

The death of a family member or friend is an extraordinarily emotional, stressful time. This stress can be compounded when you also have been asked to serve as executor of a person's estate. During the last twenty-two years I have had the privilege of representing numerous executors, most of whom had never served as executor before. There are three initial steps that an executor can take that will decrease stress and potential liability.

Getting the Right Advice

The most important step you can take is to seek appropriate help in serving as executor. You have every right (as a proper expense of the estate) to hire an attorney or other agent to help you. The right person will take the complexity out of the duties and ambiguities of being an executor, which in turn will reduce your fears, stress, and liability.

Simplifying the Process Whenever Possible

There are times when someone named as executor does not need to serve in that role to distribute the estate's assets. Many times, a decedent dies with very few assets over which the executor needs to assert authority. By doing some due diligence prior to someone officially accepting the role of executor, I have found several situations where no one needed to serve as executor—saving the estate thousands of dollars in costs.

Reducing Personal Liability by Following Some Key Rules

Hold off on paying any Bills (at least initially). If you find that you need to act as executor, one of the most counterintuitive pieces of advice I give is *not* to pay any of the decedent's debts or estate expenses until you have a handle on what assets are in the estate and what debts and expenses exist. If the estate does not have enough assets to cover all the estate expenses and debts, then there is a strict order in which debts can be paid under state law.

Protect yourself to the full extent of the law. The good news is that there are certain procedures that can be followed under state and federal law that will limit your personal liability. A prudent executor will work with an attorney to take advantage of all available methods for reducing personal liability.

Chapter 18

Keeping Current

Estate planning, much like any area of law, is constantly changing. In an effort to keep the book current, I have created a website, www. handwriteyourwill.com, where I will post any updates to this book and where I will create a Frequently Asked Questions page to discuss questions raised by the readers. And though I cannot respond directly to every reader, I will do my best to address questions on this website. I thank you for purchasing this book, and I hope that it has helped you in your own estate planning journey.

Appendix 1: Glossary

Administrator. Title for a person appointed to administer the estate where there is no will, or where there is a will, but the person being appointed was not named.

Bequeath/bequest. To leave an item of tangible personal property or cash to a person through the will.

Descendants. A person's children, grandchildren, and great-grandchildren (and further related by bloodline).

Devise. To give real property to a person through the will.

Executor/personal representative. Title for a person named in a will to administer the estate.

Heirs/heirs at law. Heirs at law are the persons who inherit an intestate estate and are designated by statute in your state.

Intestate. Means that the decedent died without a valid will.

Lapse. Where a bequest or devise in a will is not made because the person to whom the item was to pass died.

Probate. Probate is the procedure where a will is recorded or admitted to record in the court. "Probate" is sometimes used broadly to describe the administration of an estate.

Probate property. A decedent's will has power only over the decedent's probate assets. Generally, there are two types of property that make up the probate estate: (1) assets solely in the name of the decedent and (2) assets payable to the decedent's estate.

Nonprobate assets. There are many types of property that are "nonprobate" property and that pass outside the will. These are assets that pass automatically to a beneficiary at death and are not subject to the terms of the will. Some common examples of nonprobate property are (1) assets owned jointly with right of survivorship, (2) assets that have one or more designated beneficiaries (e.g., life insurance, IRAs, 401(k)s), and (3) accounts that are designated as transfer on death (TOD) or payable on death (POD).

Testate. Means that the decedent died with a valid will.

Testator. The person creating the will.

Appendix 2: Estate and Inheritance Tax Status for States That Allow Holographic Wills

States allowing holographic wills	Estate and/or inheritance tax	Notes
Alaska	No estate or inheritance tax	
Arizona	No estate or inheritance tax	
Arkansas	No estate or inheritance tax	
California	No estate or inheritance tax	
Colorado	No estate or inheritance tax	
Hawaii	Estate tax threshold $5.49 million	Equal to the federal exemption, indexed annually for inflation 0.8–16.0% tax rate
Idaho	No estate or inheritance tax	
Kentucky	Inheritance tax	0.0–16.0% tax rate
Maine	Estate tax threshold $5.49 million	Equal to the federal exemption, indexed annually for inflation 8–12% tax rate
Michigan	No estate or inheritance tax	
Mississippi	No estate or inheritance tax	
Montana	No estate or inheritance tax	
Nebraska	Inheritance tax	1.0–18.0% tax rate

Nevada	No estate or inheritance tax	
New Jersey	Estate and inheritance tax Note: estate tax repealed for deaths starting 1/1/2018	Estate tax threshold $2 million 0.8–16.0% estate tax rate 0–16% inheritance tax rate (still in effect in 2018)
North Carolina	No estate or inheritance tax	
North Dakota	No estate or inheritance tax	
Oklahoma	No estate or inheritance tax	
Pennsylvania	No estate or inheritance tax	
South Dakota	No estate or inheritance tax	
Tennessee	No estate or inheritance tax	
Texas	No estate or inheritance tax	
Utah	No estate or inheritance tax	
Virginia	No estate or inheritance tax	
West Virginia	No estate or inheritance tax	
Wyoming	No estate or inheritance tax	

Appendix 3: States That Allow Tangible Personal Property to Be Distributed by List

States allowing holographic wills	Allow transfer of tangible personal property by list?
Alaska	yes
Arizona	yes
Arkansas	yes
California	yes
Colorado	yes
Hawaii	yes
Idaho	yes
Kentucky	no
Maine	yes
Michigan	yes
Mississippi	no
Montana	yes
Nebraska	yes
Nevada	yes
New Jersey	yes
North Carolina	no
North Dakota	yes
Oklahoma	no
Pennsylvania	no
South Dakota	yes
Tennessee	no

Texas	no
Utah	yes
Virginia	yes
West Virginia	no
Wyoming	yes

Appendix 4: Uniform Transfers to Minors Act Age Limitations

States allowing holographic wills	Age(s) minor receives property under Uniform Transfers to Minors Act
Alaska	18 to 25
Arizona	21
Arkansas	18 to 21
California	18 to 25
Colorado	21
Hawaii	21
Idaho	21
Kentucky	18
Maine	18 to 21
Michigan	18 to 21
Mississippi	21
Montana	21
Nebraska	21
Nevada	18 to 25
New Jersey	18 to 21
North Carolina	18 to 21
North Dakota	21
Oklahoma	18 to 21
Pennsylvania	21 to 25
South Dakota	18
Tennessee	21 to 25
Texas	21

Utah	21
Virginia	18 to 21
West Virginia	21
Wyoming	21

Appendix 5: Powers That Can Be Incorporated under Virginia 64.2-105

The following powers, in addition to all other powers granted by law, may be incorporated in whole or in part in any will or trust instrument by reference to this section:

1. To keep and retain any or all investments and property, real, personal or mixed, including stock in the fiduciary, if the fiduciary is a corporation, in the same form as they are at the time the investments and property come into the custody of the fiduciary, regardless of the character of the investments and property, whether they are such as then would be authorized by law for investment by fiduciaries, or whether a disproportionately large part of the trust or estate remains invested in one or more types of property, for such time as the fiduciary deems best, and to dispose of such property by sale, exchange, or otherwise as and when such fiduciary deems advisable.

2. At the discretion of the fiduciary, to receive additions to the estate from any source, in cash or in kind, and to hold, administer, and distribute such additions as a part of and under the same terms and conditions as the estate then currently held.

3. To sell, assign, exchange, transfer and convey, or otherwise dispose of, any or all of the investments and property, real, personal or mixed, that are included in, or may at any time become part of the trust or estate upon such terms and

conditions as the fiduciary, in his absolute discretion, deems advisable, at either public or private sale, either for cash or deferred payments or other consideration, as the fiduciary determines. For the purpose of selling, assigning, exchanging, transferring, or conveying such investments and property, the fiduciary has the power to make, execute, acknowledge, and deliver any and all instruments of conveyance, deeds of trust, or assignments in such form and with warranties and covenants as the fiduciary deems expedient and proper; and in the event of any sale, conveyance, exchange, or other disposition of any of the trust or estate, the purchaser shall not be obligated in any way to see to the application of the purchase money or other consideration passing in connection therewith.

4. To grant, sell, transfer, exchange, purchase, or acquire options of any kind on property held by such trust or estate or acquired or to be acquired by such trust or estate or held or owned by any other person.

5. To lease any or all of the real estate that is included in or may at any time become a part of the trust or estate upon such terms and conditions as the fiduciary in his sole judgment and discretion deems advisable. Any lease made by the fiduciary may extend beyond the term of the trust or administration of the estate and, for the purpose of leasing such real estate, the fiduciary has the power to make, execute, acknowledge, and deliver any and all instruments, in such form and with such covenants and warranties as the fiduciary deems expedient and proper.

6. To vote any stocks, bonds, or other securities held by the fiduciary at any meeting of stockholders, bondholders, or other security holders, and to delegate the power to so vote to attorneys-in-fact or proxies under power of attorney, restricted or unrestricted.

7. To borrow money for such periods of time and upon such terms and conditions as to rates, maturities, renewals, and security as to the fiduciary seems advisable, including the power to borrow from the fiduciary, if the fiduciary is a bank, for the purpose of paying (i) debts, taxes, or other charges against the trust or estate or any part thereof and (ii) with prior approval of the court for any proper purpose of the trust or estate. The fiduciary has the power to mortgage or pledge such portion of the trust or estate as may be required to secure such loans and, as maker or endorser, to renew existing loans.

8. To make loans or advancements to the executor or other representative of the grantor's estate in case such executor or other representative is in need of cash with which to pay taxes, claims, or other indebtedness of the grantor's estate; but no assets acquired from a qualified retirement benefit plan under § 2039(c) of the Internal Revenue Code shall be used to make such loans or advancements, and such assets shall be segregated and held separately until all claims against the estate for debts of the decedent or claims of administration have been satisfied. Such loans or advancements may be secured or unsecured, and the trustee is not liable in any way for any loss resulting to the trust or estate by reason of the exercise of this authority.

9. To compromise, adjust, arbitrate, sue on or defend, abandon, or otherwise deal with and settle claims in favor of or against the trust or estate as the fiduciary deems best, and his decision is conclusive.

10. To make distributions in cash or in kind or partly in each at valuations to be determined by the fiduciary, whose decision as to values shall be conclusive.

11. To repair, alter, improve, renovate, reconstruct, or demolish any of the buildings on the real estate held by the fiduciary

and to construct such buildings and improvements thereon as the fiduciary in his discretion deems advisable.

12. To employ and compensate, out of the principal or income, or both as to the fiduciary seems proper, agents, accountants, brokers, attorneys-in-fact, attorneys-at-law, tax specialists, licensed real estate brokers, licensed salesmen, and other assistants and advisers deemed by the fiduciary to be needful for the proper administration of the trust or estate, and to do so without liability for any neglect, omission, misconduct, or default of any such agent or professional representative provided he was selected and retained with reasonable care.

13. To rely upon any affidavit, certificate, letter, notice, telegram, or other paper or upon any telephone conversation believed by the fiduciary to be genuine and upon any other evidence believed by the fiduciary to be sufficient, and to be protected and held harmless for all payments or distributions required to be made hereunder if made in good faith and without actual notice or knowledge of the changed condition or status of any person receiving payments or other distributions upon a condition.

14. To retain any interest held by the fiduciary in any business, whether as a stockholder or security holder of a corporation, a partner, a sole proprietor, or otherwise, for any length of time, without limitations, solely at the risk of the trust or estate and without liability on the part of the fiduciary for any losses resulting therefrom; including the power to (i) participate in the conduct of such business and take or delegate to others discretionary power to take any action with respect to its management and affairs that an individual could take as the owner of such business, including the voting of stock and the determination of any or all questions of policy; (ii) participate in any incorporation, reorganization, merger, consolidation, recapitalization, or liquidation of the business;

(iii) invest additional capital in, subscribe to additional stock or securities of, and loan money or credit with or without security to, such business out of the trust or estate property; (iv) elect or employ as directors, officers, employees, or agents of such business, and compensate, any persons, including the fiduciary or a director, officer, or agent of the fiduciary; (v) accept as correct financial or other statements rendered by the business from time to time as to its conditions and operations except when having actual notice to the contrary; (vi) regard the business as an entity separate from the trust or estate with no duty to account to any court as to its operations; (vii) deal with and act for the business in any capacity, including any banking or trust capacity and the loaning of money out of the fiduciary's own funds, and to be compensated therefor; and (viii) sell or liquidate such interest or any part thereof at any time. If any business shall be unincorporated, contractual and tort liabilities arising out of such business shall be satisfied, first, out of the business, and second, out of the trust or estate; but in no event shall there be a liability of the fiduciary, and if the fiduciary is held liable, the fiduciary is entitled to indemnification from, first, the business, and second, the trust or estate. The fiduciary is entitled to such additional compensation as is commensurate with the time, effort, and responsibility involved in his performance of services with respect to such business. Such compensation for services rendered to the business may be paid by the fiduciary from the business or from other assets or from both as the fiduciary, in his discretion, determines to be advisable; however, the amount of such additional compensation is subject to the final approval of the court.

15. To do all other acts and things not inconsistent with the provisions of the will or trust in which these powers are incorporated that the fiduciary deems necessary or desirable for

the proper management of the trusts herein created, in the same manner and to the same extent as an individual could do with respect to his own property.

16. To hold property in the fiduciary's name or in the name of nominees.

17. During the minority, incapacity, or the disability of any beneficiary, and in the sole discretion of the fiduciary, to distribute income and principal to the beneficiary in any of the following ways: (i) directly to the beneficiary; (ii) to a relative, friend, guardian, conservator, or committee, to be expended by such person for the education, maintenance, support, or benefit of the beneficiary; (iii) by the fiduciary expending the same for the education, maintenance, support, or benefit of the beneficiary; (iv) to an adult person or bank authorized to exercise trust powers as custodian for a minor beneficiary under the Uniform Transfers to Minors Act (§ 64.2-1900 et seq.) to be held by such custodian under the terms of such act; or (v) to an adult person or bank authorized to exercise trust powers as custodial trustee for a beneficiary who is incapacitated as defined in § 64.2-900, under the Uniform Custodial Trust Act (§ 64.2-900 et seq.) to be held as custodial trustee under the terms of such act.

18. To continue and carry on any farming operation transferred to the fiduciary and to operate such farms and any other farm which may be acquired, including the power to (i) operate the farm with hired labor, tenants, or sharecroppers; (ii) hire a farm manager or a professional farm management service to supervise the farming operations; (iii) lease or rent the farm for cash or for a share of the crops; (iv) purchase or otherwise acquire farm machinery, equipment, and livestock; (v) construct, repair, and improve farm buildings of all sorts necessary, in the fiduciary's judgment, for the operation of the farm; (vi) make loans or advances or to obtain loans

or advances from any source, including the fiduciary at the prevailing rate of interest for farm purposes including for production, harvesting, or marketing, for the construction, repair, or improvement of farm buildings, or for the purchase of farm machinery, equipment, or livestock; (vii) employ approved soil conservation practices in order to conserve, improve, and maintain the fertility and productivity of the soil; (viii) protect, manage, and improve the timber and forest on the farm and sell the timber and forest products when it is to the best interest of the estate or trust; (ix) ditch and drain damp or wet fields and areas of the farm when needed; (x) engage in livestock production, if it is deemed advisable, and to construct such fences and buildings and plant such pastures and crops as may be necessary to carry on a livestock program; (xi) execute contracts, notes, and chattel mortgages relating to agriculture with the Commodity Credit Corporation, the United States Secretary of Agriculture, or any other officer or agency of the federal or state government, to enter into acreage reduction agreements, to make soil conservation commitments, and to do all acts necessary to cooperate with any governmental agricultural program; and (xii) in general, employ the methods of carrying on the farming operation that are in common use by the community in which the farm is located. As the duties that the fiduciary is requested to assume with respect to farming operations may considerably enlarge and increase the fiduciary's usual responsibility and work as fiduciary, the fiduciary is entitled to such additional reasonable compensation as is commensurate with the time, effort, and responsibility involved in his performance of such services.

19. To purchase and hold life insurance policies on the life of any beneficiary, or any person in whom the beneficiary has an insurable interest, and pay the premiums thereon out of income or principal as the fiduciary deems appropriate; provided,

however, that the decision of the beneficiary of any trust otherwise meeting the requirements of § 2056(b)(5) of the Internal Revenue Code of 1954, as amended, shall control in respect to the purchase or holding of a life insurance policy by the trustee of such trust.

20. To make any election, including any election permitted by statutes enacted after the date of execution of the will or trust instrument, authorized under any law requiring, or relating to the requirement for, payment of any taxes or assessments on assets or income of the estate or in connection with any fiduciary capacity, regardless of whether any property or income is received by or is under the control of the fiduciary, including, elections concerning the timing of payment of any such tax or assessment, the valuation of any property subject to any such tax or assessment, and the alternative use of items of deduction in computing any tax or assessment.

21. To comply with environmental law:

    a. To inspect property held by the fiduciary, including interests in sole proprietorships, partnerships, or corporations and any assets owned by any such business enterprise, for the purpose of determining compliance with environmental law affecting such property and to respond to a change in, or any actual or threatened violation of, any environmental law affecting property held by the fiduciary;

    b. To take, on behalf of the estate or trust, any action necessary to respond to a change in, or prevent, abate, or otherwise remedy any actual or threatened violation of, any environmental law affecting property held by the fiduciary, either before or after the initiation of an enforcement action by any governmental body;

    c. To refuse to accept property in trust if the fiduciary determines that any property to be transferred to the trust either is contaminated by any hazardous substance or is being used or has been used for any activity directly or indirectly involving any hazardous substance which could result in liability to the trust or otherwise impair the value of the assets held therein;

    d. To deny any power granted by any document, statute, or rule of law that, in the sole discretion of the fiduciary, may cause the fiduciary to incur personal liability under any environmental law; and

    e. To charge the cost of any inspection, review, abatement, response, cleanup, or remedial action authorized herein against the income or principal of the trust or estate.

22. To resign as fiduciary if the fiduciary reasonably believes that there is or may be a conflict of interest between him in his fiduciary capacity and in his individual capacity because of potential claims or liabilities which may be asserted against him on behalf of the trust or estate because of the type or condition of assets held therein.

    C. For the purposes of this section, unless the will or trust instrument expresses a contrary intention, the incorporation by reference of powers enumerated by this statute shall refer to those powers existing at the time of death and reference to powers under the Uniform Gifts to Minors Act in an instrument executed prior to July 1, 1989, shall be construed to refer to the Uniform Transfers to Minors Act (§ 64.2-1900 et seq.).

Appendix 6: Powers Found in WVA Section 44-5A-3

The following powers may be incorporated by reference as provided in section two of this article:

(a) Retain original property. -- To retain for such time as the fiduciary considers advisable any property, real or personal, which the fiduciary may receive, even though the retention of such property by reason of its character, amount, proportion to the total estate or otherwise would not be appropriate for the fiduciary apart from this provision.

(b) Sell and exchange property. -- To sell, exchange, give options upon, partition or otherwise dispose of any property or interest therein which the fiduciary may hold from time to time, with or without order of court, at public or private sale or otherwise, upon such terms and conditions, including credit, and for such consideration as the fiduciary considers advisable, and to transfer and convey the property or interest therein which is at the disposal of the fiduciary, in fee simple absolute or otherwise, free of all trust; and the party dealing with the fiduciary is not under a duty to follow the proceeds or other consideration received by the fiduciary from such sale or exchange.

(c) Invest and reinvest. -- To invest and reinvest, as the fiduciary considers advisable, in stocks (common or preferred), bonds, debentures, notes, mortgages or other securities, in or outside the United States; in insurance contracts on the life of any beneficiary or of any person in whom a beneficiary has an insurable interest, or in annuity contracts for any beneficiary, in any real or personal property, in investment trusts; in participations in common trust funds, and generally in such property as the fiduciary considers advisable, even though such investment is not of the character approved by applicable law but for this provision.

(d) Invest without diversification. -- To make investments which cause a greater proportion of the total property held by the fiduciary to be invested in investments of one type or of one company than would be considered appropriate for the fiduciary apart from this provision.

(e) Continue business. -- To the extent and upon such terms and conditions and for such periods of time as the fiduciary considers necessary or advisable, to continue or participate in the operation of any business or other enterprise, whatever its form of organization, including, but not limited to, the power:

1. To effect incorporation, dissolution, or other change in the form of the organization of the business or enterprise;
2. To dispose of any interest therein or acquire the interest of others therein;
3. To contribute thereto or invest therein additional capital or to lend money thereto, in any such case upon such terms and conditions as the fiduciary approves from time to time;
4. To determine whether the liabilities incurred in the conduct of the business are to be chargeable solely to the part of the estate or trust set aside for use in the business or to the estate or trust as a whole; and
5. In all cases in which the fiduciary is required to file accounts in any court or in any other public office, it is not necessary to itemize receipts and disbursements and distributions of

property but it is sufficient for the fiduciary to show in the account a single figure or consolidation of figures, and the fiduciary is permitted to account for money and property received from the business and any payments made to the business in lump sum without itemization.

(f) Form corporation or other entity. -- To form a corporation or other entity and to transfer, assign, and convey to such corporation or entity all or any part of the estate or of any trust property in exchange for the stock, securities or obligations of any such corporation or entity, and to continue to hold such stock and securities and obligations.

(g) Operate farm. -- To continue any farming operation received by the fiduciary pursuant to the will or other instrument and to do any and all things considered advisable by the fiduciary in the management and maintenance of such farm and the production and marketing of crops and dairy, poultry, livestock, orchard and forest products including, but not limited to, the following powers:

1. To operate the farm with hired labor, tenants or sharecroppers;
2. To lease or rent the farm for cash or for a share of the crops;
3. To purchase or otherwise acquire farm machinery and equipment and livestock;
4. To construct, repair and improve farm buildings of all kinds needed in the fiduciary's judgment, for the operation of the farm;
5. To make or obtain loans or advances at the prevailing rate or rates of interest for farm purposes such as for production, harvesting, or marketing, or for the construction, repair, or improvement of farm buildings or for the purchase of farm machinery or equipment or livestock;
6. To employ approved soil conservation practices in order to conserve, improve and maintain the fertility and productivity of the soil;

7. To protect, manage and improve the timber and forest on the farm and sell the timber and forest products when it is to the best interest of the estate;

8. To ditch, dam and drain damp or wet fields and areas of the farm when and where needed;

9. To engage in the production of livestock, poultry or dairy products, and to construct such fences and buildings and plant such pastures and crops as may be necessary to carry on such operations;

10. To market the products of the farm; and

11. In general, to employ good husbandry in the farming operation.

(h) Manage real property. --

1. To improve, manage, protect and subdivide any real property;

2. To dedicate or withdraw from dedication parks, streets, highways or alleys;

3. To terminate any subdivision or part thereof;

4. To borrow money for the purposes authorized by this subdivision for such periods of time and upon such terms and conditions as to rates, maturities and renewals as the fiduciary considers advisable and to mortgage or otherwise encumber any such property or part thereof, whether in possession or reversion;

5. To lease any such property or part thereof to commence at the present or in the future, upon such terms and conditions, including options to renew or purchase, and for such period or periods of time as the fiduciary considers advisable although such period or periods may extend beyond the duration of the trust or the administration of the estate involved;

6. To make coal, gravel, sand, oil, gas and other mineral leases, contracts, licenses, conveyances or grants of every nature and

kind which are lawful in the jurisdiction in which such property lies;

7. To manage and improve timber and forests on such property, to sell the timber and forest products, and to make grants, leases, and contracts with respect thereto;

8. To modify, renew or extend leases;

9. To employ agents to rent and collect rents;

10. To create easements and release, convey, or assign any right, title, or interest with respect to any easement on such property or part thereof;

11. To erect, repair or renovate any building or other improvement on such property, and to remove or demolish any building or other improvement, in whole or in part; and

12. To deal with any such property and every part thereof in all other ways and for such other purposes or considerations as it would be lawful for any person owning the same to deal with such property either in the same or in different ways from those specified elsewhere in this subdivision (h).

(i) Pay taxes and expenses. -- To pay taxes, assessments, compensation of the fiduciary, and other expenses incurred in the collection, care, administration, and protection of the trust or estate.

(j) Receive additional property. -- To receive additional property from any source and administer such additional property as a portion of the appropriate trust or estate under the management of the fiduciary but the fiduciary is not required to receive such property without his or her consent.

(k) Deal with other trusts. -- In dealing with one or more fiduciaries:

1. To sell property, real or personal, to, or to exchange property with, the trustee of any trust which the decedent or the settlor

or his spouse or any child of his shall have created, for such estates and upon such terms and conditions as to sale price, terms of payment, and security as the fiduciary considers advisable; and the fiduciary is under no duty to follow the proceeds of any such sale; and

2. To borrow money for such periods of time and upon such terms and conditions as to rates, maturities, renewals and securities as the fiduciary considers advisable from any trust created by the decedent, his spouse, or any child of his, for the purpose of paying debts of the decedent, taxes, the costs of the administration of the estate, and like charges against the estate, or any part thereof, or discharging the liability of any fiduciary thereof and to mortgage, pledge or otherwise encumber such portion of the estate or any trust as may be required to secure such loan or loans and to renew such loans.

(l) Borrow money. -- To borrow money for such periods of time and upon such terms and conditions as to rates, maturities, renewals, and security as the fiduciary considers advisable, including the power of a corporate fiduciary to borrow from its own banking department, for the purpose of paying debts, taxes, or other charges against the estate or any trust, or any part thereof, and to mortgage, pledge or otherwise encumber such portion of the estate or any trust as may be required to secure such loan or loans; and to renew existing loans either as maker or endorser.

(m) Make advances. -- To advance money for the protection of the trust or estate, and for all expenses, losses and liabilities sustained in the administration of the trust or estate or because of the holding or ownership of any trust or estate assets, for which advances with any interest the fiduciary shall have a lien on the assets of the trust or estate as against a beneficiary.

(n) Vote shares. -- To vote shares of stock owned by the estate or any trust at stockholder's meetings in person or by special, limited, or general proxy, with or without power of substitution.

(o) Register in name of nominee. -- To hold a security in the name of a nominee or in other form without disclosure of the fiduciary relationship so that title to the security may pass by delivery, but the fiduciary is liable for any act of the nominee in connection with the stock so held.

(p) Exercise options, rights and privileges. -- To exercise all options, rights, and privileges to convert stocks, bonds, debentures, notes, mortgages, or other property into other stocks, bonds, debentures, notes, mortgages, or other property; to subscribe for other or additional stocks, bonds, debentures, notes, mortgages, or other property; and to hold such stocks, bonds, debentures, notes, mortgages, or other property so acquired as investments of the estate or trust so long as the fiduciary considers advisable.

(q) Participate in reorganizations. -- To unite with other owners of property similar to any which may be held at any time in the decedent's estate or in any trusts in carrying out any plan for the consolidation or merger, dissolution or liquidation, foreclosure, lease, or sale of the property, incorporation or reincorporation, reorganization or readjustment of the capital or financial structure of any corporation, company or association the securities of which may form any portion of an estate or trust; to become and serve as a member of a stockholders or bondholders protective committee; to deposit securities in accordance with any plan agreed upon; to pay any assessments, expenses, or sums of money that may be required for the protection or furtherance of the interest of the distributees of an estate or beneficiaries of any trust with reference to any such plan; and to receive as investments of an estate or any trust any securities issued as a result of the execution of such plan.

(r) Reduce interest rates. -- To reduce the interest rate from time to time on any obligation, whether secured or unsecured, constituting a part of an estate or trust.

(s) Renew and extend obligations. -- To continue any obligation, whether secured or unsecured, upon and after maturity with or without renewal or extension upon such terms as the fiduciary considers advisable, without regard to the value of the security, if any, at the time of such continuance.

(t) Foreclose and bid in. -- To foreclose, as an incident to the collection of any bond, note or other obligation, any mortgage, deed of trust, or other lien securing such bond, note or other obligation, and to bid in the property at such foreclosure sale, or to acquire the property by deed from the mortgagor or obligor without foreclosure; and to retain the property so bid in or taken over without foreclosure.

(u) Insure. -- To carry such insurance coverage, including public liability, for such hazards and in such amounts, either in stock companies or in mutual companies, as the fiduciary considers advisable.

(v) Collect. -- To collect, receive and receipt for rents, issues, profits, and income of an estate or trust.

(w) Litigate, compromise or abandon. -- To compromise, adjust, arbitrate, sue on or defend, abandon, or otherwise deal with and settle claims in favor of or against the estate or trust as the fiduciary considers advisable, and the fiduciary's decision is conclusive between the fiduciary and the beneficiaries of the estate or trust and the person against or for whom the claim is asserted, in the absence of fraud by such persons; and in the absence of fraud, bad faith or gross negligence of the fiduciary, is conclusive between the fiduciary and the beneficiaries of the estate or trust.

(x) Employ and compensate agents, etc. -- To employ and compensate, out of income or principal or both and in such proportion as the fiduciary considers advisable, persons considered by the fiduciary needful to advise or assist in the proper settlement of the estate or administration of any trust, including, but not limited to, agents, accountants, brokers, attorneys-at-law, attorneys-in-fact, investment brokers, rental agents, realtors, appraisers, and tax specialists; and to do so without liability for any neglect, omission, misconduct, or default of such agent or representative provided he or she was selected and retained with due care on the part of the fiduciary.

(y) Acquire and hold property of two or more trusts undivided. -- To acquire, receive, hold and retain the principal of several trusts created by a single instrument undivided until division becomes necessary in order to make distributions; to hold, manage, invest, reinvest, and account for the several shares or parts of shares by appropriate entries in the fiduciary's books of account, and to allocate to each share or part of share its proportionate part of all receipts and expenses: Provided, That the provisions of this subdivision do not defer the vesting in possession of any share or part of share of the estate or trust.

(z) Establish and maintain reserves. -- To set up proper and reasonable reserves for taxes, assessments, insurance premiums, depreciation, obsolescence, amortization, depletion of mineral or timber properties, repairs, improvements, and general maintenance of buildings or other property out of rents, profits, or other income received; and to set up reserves also for the equalization of payments to or for beneficiaries: Provided, That the provisions of this subdivision do not affect the ultimate interests of beneficiaries in such reserves.

(aa) Distribute in cash or kind. -- To make distribution of capital assets of the estate or trust in kind or in cash, or partially in kind and partially in cash, in divided or undivided interests, as the fiduciary finds to be most practicable and for the best interests of the distributees; and to determine the value of capital assets for the purpose of making distribution thereof if and when there be more than one distributee thereof, which determination shall be binding upon the distributees unless clearly capricious, erroneous and inequitable: Provided, That the fiduciary may not exercise any power under this subdivision unless the fiduciary holds title to or an interest in the property to be distributed and is required or authorized to make distribution thereof.

(bb) Pay to or for minors or incompetents. -- To make payments in money, or in property in lieu of money, to or for a minor or incompetent in any one or more of the following ways:

1. Directly to such minor or incompetent;
2. To apply directly in payment for the support, maintenance, education, and medical, surgical, hospital, or other institutional care of such minor or incompetent;
3. To the legal or natural guardian of such minor or incompetent;
4. To any other person, whether or not appointed guardian of the person by any court, who does, in fact, have the care and custody of the person of such minor or incompetent.

The fiduciary is not under any duty to see to the application of the payments so made, if the fiduciary exercised due care in the selection of the person, including the minor or incompetent, to whom such payments were made; and the receipt of such person is full acquittance to the fiduciary.

(cc) Apportion and allocate receipts and expenses. -- Where not otherwise provided by statute to determine:

1. What is principal and what is income of any estate or trust and to allocate or apportion receipts and expenses as between

principal and income in the exercise of the fiduciary's discretion, and, by way of illustration and not limitation of the fiduciary's discretion, to charge premiums on securities purchased at a premium against principal or income or partly against each;

2. Whether to apply stock dividends and other noncash dividends to income or principal or apportion them as the fiduciary considers advisable; and

3. What expenses, costs, taxes (other than estate, inheritance, and succession taxes and other governmental charges) shall be charged against principal or income or apportioned between principal and income and in what proportions.

(dd) Make contracts and execute instruments. -- To make contracts and to execute instruments, under seal or otherwise, as may be necessary in the exercise of the powers herein granted.

(ee) The foregoing powers are limited as follows for any trust which shall be classified as a "private foundation" as that term is defined by section 509 of the Internal Revenue Code of 1954 or corresponding provisions of any subsequent federal tax laws (including each nonexempt charitable trust described in section 4947(a)(1) of the code which is treated as a private foundation) or nonexempt split-interest trust described in section 4947(a)(2) of the Internal Revenue Code of 1954 or corresponding provisions of any subsequent federal tax laws (but only to the extent that section 508(e) of the code is applicable to such nonexempt split-interest trust under section 4947(a)(2)):

1. The fiduciary shall make distributions of such amounts, for each taxable year, at such time and in such manner as not to become subject to the tax imposed by section 4942 of the Internal Revenue Code of 1954, or corresponding provisions of any subsequent federal tax laws;

2. No fiduciary may engage in any act of self-dealing as defined in section 4941(d) of the Internal Revenue Code of 1954, or corresponding provisions of any subsequent federal tax laws;

3. No fiduciary may retain any excess business holdings as defined in section 4943(c) of the Internal Revenue Code of 1954, or corresponding provisions of any subsequent federal tax laws;

4. No fiduciary may make any investments in such manner as to subject the trust to tax under section 4944 of the Internal Revenue Code of 1954, or corresponding provisions of any subsequent federal tax laws;(5) No fiduciary may make any taxable expenditures as defined in section 4945(e) of the Internal Revenue Code of 1954, or corresponding provisions of any subsequent federal tax laws.

Appendix 7: What Your Survivors Should Know

The following checklist may be used as a guide to ensure your survivors are able to carry out your wishes. By leaving behind a plan that clearly indicates your wishes concerning a funeral or memorial service, the names of your advisers, and where your important documents are kept, you can make life easier for your survivors.

I.   Funeral and Burial Information

Full name: _____

Address: _____

Date of birth: _____

Place of birth: _____

Family Information

Spouse   _____ Date of marriage: _____

Birthplace: City_____ State_____

Deceased?_____ Year_____

Parents

Father's name: _____

Address, if living: _____

Birthplace: City_____ State_____

Deceased?_____ Year_____

Mother's maiden name: _____

Address, if living: _____

Birthplace: City_____ State_____

Deceased?_____ Year_____

Children

Name	Date of birth	Address
_____	_____	_____
_____	_____	_____
_____	_____	_____
_____	_____	_____
_____	_____	_____
_____	_____	_____

Grandchildren

Name	Date of birth	Address
_____	_____	_____
_____	_____	_____
_____	_____	_____
_____	_____	_____
_____	_____	_____
_____	_____	_____
_____	_____	_____

Brothers and Sisters

Name	Date of birth	Address
_____	_____	_____
_____	_____	_____
_____	_____	_____
_____	_____	_____
_____	_____	_____
_____	_____	_____
_____	_____	_____

Education

School(s)	Degree(s)	Year

Community Information

Church: _____

_____

Clubs and fraternal and military organizations: _____

_____

_____

Civic organizations: _____

_____

_____

Offices held and recognitions received: _____

_____

_____

Military service: _____

_____

Rank attained   Unit   Date entered   Date discharged

_____

_____

Employment/business: _____

_____

Firm   Since (date)   Present position

_____

Other items of interest concerning business or life history:

_____

_____

_____

Corporate directorates and offices held: _____

_____

_____

Funeral Arrangements

Considerations

Choose type of disposition and ceremony.

- o You can choose a ceremonial service, religious or secular, with the body present or with cremation.

If you wish to prepay for your funeral costs, make sure you know exactly what you are purchasing and what will happen if the funeral organization goes out of business.

- o Keep copies of documents given to you when you make the prearrangements.
- o Veterans, service members, and their dependents

can be buried in a national cemetery for free.
If buried elsewhere, veterans who at the time
of death were entitled to receive VA disability
payments can receive an allowance toward
funeral and burial expenses. This allowance may
be greater if the death was related to military
service or if it occurred in a VA hospital. Other
benefits may include a ceremonial American
flag, a headstone, and a presidential memorial
certificate. Make sure your family is aware of
these benefits, how to get them, and what your
preferences are.

I wish: Calling hours:

☐   No funeral service   ☐ At funeral home

☐   Memorial service   ☐   At my home

☐   Funeral service   ☐ No calling hours

Prepaid? _____

Church: _____

Mortuary: _____

Home: _____

Mausoleum chapel: _____

Services

Clergyman/rabbi: _____

Special scripture or other readings: _____

Special music: _____

Flowers? _____

Donation to organization in lieu of flowers? _____

Which organization? _____

Requested pallbearers: _____

_____

_____

Any club or fraternal, civic, or military organizations you wish to have assist with your service?

_____

_____

Preferences for stone or marker? _____

_____

Any special inscription or epitaph? _____

Any arrangements already made with: _____

Funeral home: _____

Marker manufacturer: _____

Cemetery: _____

Obituaries—preference for printing in following papers:

_____

_____

Burial Arrangements

I prefer:

☐ Burial ☐ Cremation

☐ Need to purchase ☐ Wishes for my ashes:

☐ Cemetery lot _____

☐ Already own _____

Where? _____

Lot #? _____

Funeral home: _____

Address: _____

Other preferences:

_____

Any jewelry, clothing, or other items you wish to be buried with or not buried with?

II. Estate Administration

Estate planning attorney

Name: _____

Address: _____

Telephone #: _____

Email: _____

Accountant _____

Name: _____

Address: _____

Telephone #: _____

Email: _____

Insurance agent

Name: _____

Address: _____

Telephone #: _____

Email: _____

Investment adviser

Name: _____

Address: _____

Telephone #: _____

Email: _____

Location of original estate planning documents: _____

Executor(s) named: _____

Guardian(s) named: _____

III.   Location of Key Documents

Item   Location

Item	Location
☐ Birth certificate	
☐ Marriage license	
☐ Financial statements Including those from banks, brokerage houses, and credit card and insurance agencies	
☐ Tax returns	
☐ Unpaid credit and utility bills	
☐ Deeds to real estate	
☐ Titles on property and cars	
☐ Mortgage payment information	
☐ Auto, home, and life insurance policies	
☐ Prearranged funeral contract	
☐ Veterans Affairs identification	
☐ Key to safe deposit box or combination to safe	
☐ Passwords for online accounts	

IV. Accounts

A. Cash (bank accounts, money market funds, CDs, etc.)

Financial institution	Account number

B. Stocks, bonds, mutual funds, and other investments

Financial institution	Account number

C. Life insurance policies

Insurance company	Policy number	Face amount
		$

D. IRA, Keogh, 401(k), and other investment plans

Financial institution	Account number

E. Your home and other real estate

Property location	How titled

F. Ownership of businesses, partnerships, or other closely held assets

Type of entity	Interest held

Printed in the United States
By Bookmasters